Costume Design
for Performance

Costume Design for Performance

Bettina John

THE CROWOOD PRESS

First published in 2021 by
The Crowood Press Ltd
Ramsbury, Marlborough
Wiltshire SN8 2HR

enquiries@crowood.com

www.crowood.com

British Library Cataloguing-in-Publication Data
A catalogue record for this book is available from the British Library.

ISBN 978 1 78500 927 3

Front cover image: Costume design and make by set and costume designer Bettina John for 'Broken Dreams' (2019, Belinda Evangelica) (Headpiece and beadwork by Anna Kompaniets).

Back cover images: (left and right) costume illustrations by Phillip Boutté Jr for Black Panther (2018, directed by Ryan Coogler, costume design by Ruth E Carter); (centre) PING (2014, Daphne Karstens).

Frontispiece: costume design by costume designer and maker Sophie Ruth Donaldson for Rubby Sucky Forge (2020, by Eve Stainton with Joseph Funnel and Gaby Agis), photograph by Anne Tetzlaff.

Typeset by Simon and Sons

Cover design by Maggie Mellett

Printed and bound in India by Parksons Graphics Pvt. Ltd.

CONTENTS

PREFACE

Since embarking on the writing of this book one year ago, I have discovered far more about costume than I could ever have imagined. I knew from the outset that I wanted to include as many voices from my community as possible, but I never dreamed that I would get the chance to speak to so many professionals and receive this extent of valuable insight. The generosity I experienced is exemplary of the industry and the people who work within it. It is a creative community that offers a place to everybody who shows the necessary commitment and passion. The industry welcomed me in after I had graduated from a fashion design degree course and gave me a platform to express myself, while earning a living. Granted, establishing myself as a designer entailed an enormous amount of work, but truly creative work is seldom easy. I have thoroughly enjoyed the journey from graduation to where I am today, despite the bumps and hurdles along the way. I have always continued to learn and gain further qualifications, including a Master's degree in Theatre Design, a series of short courses and a lot of on-the-job training in professional, yet welcoming environments. Several professionals helped me throughout this journey and without them I could not have developed into the designer I am now.

My aim is that this book reflects the community to which I belong, rather than acting as a response to literature on the subjects touched on within the book. I have personally worked predominantly in

costume design for theatre, opera and dance; but I wanted to include some of the parallels and departures from film. I interviewed and consulted numerous professionals to get a good grasp of how the theatre and film industries function today. In combination with my own experience working as a costume designer, I was confident that I could assemble a useful and informative introduction to the process of designing costume for performance. However, writing a compact introduction to such a vast field as costume turned out to be a bigger challenge than I imagined.

The drawings and documents included in this book are contributions by a variety of designers and artists from the United Kingdom, Germany, France, The Netherlands, Belgium, Spain, the USA, Brazil, Russia, Greece and Australia. They allow the reader an exclusive insight into an otherwise rather private process. It allows the reader a deeper understanding of the design process and it underlines the uniqueness of each and every designer and their methodology. In the process of finding contributors and carrying out interviews for this book, I became increasingly aware of this. I tested some of the ideas for the book with a group of costume professionals online, only to realize that each costume professional has their own unique perspective on the industry and that there is no single correct interpretation. Every conversation I had confirmed this, while also indicating that there is still a substantial amount of overlap and similarities. These shared methods and understandings that most professionals were able to agree on, filtered through my own experience and have formed the basis of this book.

An introduction into the world of costume can only touch the surface of the various aspects that

OPPOSITE: 'PING' (2014, costume and concept: Daphne Karstens; performer: Lorraine Smith; choreographer: Angela Woodhouse; lighting designer: Neil Brinkworth; sound designer: Nik Kennedy; make-up and hair: Goshka Topolska; photographer: Alex Traylen)

costume encompasses. Each aspect deserves its own discourse, but this is, sadly, not possible within a single publication. I must admit, I got regularly carried away conversing with other professionals, only to realize that I had to reduce hour-long conversations into short, poignant paragraphs. I encourage the reader to use this book as an entry point and to continue reading about this wonderful field and the specific aspects that interest them.

My work as a designer has allowed me to travel and see a variety of approaches to theatre-making. It has allowed me insights into the industry as it operates in various other countries, such as Germany, the USA, Brazil and Russia. However, this book is written from the perspective of the industry in the United Kingdom. Many similarities, but also some differences, exist between the industry here and in other Western European countries and the United States, particularly with regard to the infrastructure, such as costume roles, the unions and fees. However, the design process itself is always more dependent on the individual designer rather than the country in which they operate. As such, the advice given in this book, and the suggestions made, could be helpful to any aspiring costume designer, no matter where they are located on the globe.

My hope is to inspire early career designers and those that aspire to becoming designers within the theatre and film industry. I hope to offer students and graduates advice on how to become better designers and how to progress within the industry. I hope to answer many of the questions that I receive regularly from my students. I hope to give tutors and teachers a solid handbook that they can rely on when discussing costume as part of their curriculum. I hope to give all costume enthusiasts an insight into the world of costume. Above all, I hope to represent this industry in the best possible way.

ACKNOWLEDGEMENTS

CONTRIBUTORS AND INTERVIEWEES

Anna Kompaniets | Artist | Designer

Cher Potter | Designer | Researcher | Curator

Chiara Stephenson | Stage and costume designer

Christopher Oram | Set and costume designer

Clemens Leander | Costume designer and supervisor

Daphne Karstens | Wearable sculpture artist

Dione Occhipinti | Fashion stylist

E. Mallin Parry | Set and costume designer | Researcher

Fiona Watts | Scenographer

Florence Meredith | Costume designer and maker

Frances Morris | Costume designer and maker

Henriette Hübschmann | Set and costume designer

Hannah Calascione | Theatre director

Jerome Bourdin | Set and costume designer

Julia Burbach | Opera director

Julia Schnittger | Set and costume designer

Laura Iochins Grisci | Designer

Louise Gray | Multi-disciplinary designer

Lex Wood | Costume designer for film | assistant costume designer for film

Michael Grandage | Theatre director and producer

Matthew Xia | Theatre director

Nadia Lakhani | Designer and Linbury Prize Mentor

Natasha Mackmurdie | Costume supervisor

Neil Barry Moss | Director and costume designer

Noémie Laffargue | Costume designer

Phillip Boutté Jr | Concept artist

Sophie Ruth Donaldson | Costume designer and maker

Takis | Set and costume designer

Yann Seabra | Set and costume designer

IMAGE CONTRIBUTORS

Adam Nee | Set and costume designer

Bek Palmer | Set and costume designer

Brad Caleb Lee | Visual dramaturge | Designer

Brenda Mejia | Costume designer

Elizabeth Real | Costume designer and maker

English National Opera costume department

Eva Buryakovsky | Costume Designer

Evelien Van Camp | Costume designer and maker

Frankie Bradshaw | Theatre designer

Jason Southgate | Set and costume designer

Jody Broom | Student of the UAL Costume Design for Performance short course 2020

Jocquillin Shaunté Nayoan | Fashion Illustrator and Costume Designer

Laura Belzin | Fashion designer

Maryna Gradnova | Costume designer

Megan Stilwell | Costume designer and maker

Nicky Shaw | Set and costume designer

Paulina Knol | Costume designer

Rebeca Tejedor Duran | Costume designer

Sarah Bottomley | Costume designer

Stephanie Overs | Designer

Viola Borsos | Costume designer

Ysa Dora Abba | Designer

INTRODUCTION

WHY WORK IN COSTUME?

The world of costume is vast and offers endless opportunities for creative people and artists to express themselves and to work collaboratively within small, medium and large teams. The world of costume offers anybody interested in the field a place. It allows an aspiring costume professional to carve out a highly personal career and work in exactly the way they desire. This can be challenging, but it is absolutely possible, and thousands of costume professionals have achieved just this. The most important question an aspiring costume designer needs to ask themselves is why they want to be one, what sort of projects they want to be involved in and what sort of designer they want to be. A strong sense of purpose and the right work with a message the costume designer really cares about will get them through the more challenging times, which most certainly need to be expected when entering this industry. Once having found the right place within this world, it is one of the most rewarding, most enjoyable and most exciting professions or occupations there is. The sheer number of options available to a costume professional is astounding, as well as overwhelming at times. This book will give a thorough, yet clear insight into the different pathways available to an aspiring costume professional in general, while focusing on the role of the costume designer in particular.

WHO IS THIS BOOK FOR?

This book is an introduction to the world of costume and the role of the costume designer for anybody interested in the field and profession. It can act as a sourcebook for an aspiring costume designer, somebody training to become a costume professional, studying on a degree, short course or, indeed, on their own terms, or considering training. While giving concrete examples and detailed descriptions of various scenarios and processes, this book went through a rigorous editing process, with the aim to remain as clear and simple as possible, while not taking away from the complexity of the field of costume. Topics are covered from the perspective of the role of the costume designer, resulting in a reduced coverage of the work of other costume roles and aspects, which all deserve their own book. With the focus on the design process and how to become a good designer and sustain a career as a designer, this book will be useful for people from around the world. However, some information found in this book is specific to the United Kingdom and will, therefore, be particularly useful for aspiring designers wanting to work in the United Kingdom or places operating in a similar way.

WHY WRITE A BOOK LIKE THIS?

The role of the costume designer has undergone many changes over the decades of its existence and is not quite what it used to be when it started to develop in the middle of the twentieth century. The role of the costume designer grew out of a team initially less focused on design and more on providing a show with costumes and looking after them. Since then, this team has undergone fundamental changes and seen the development of numerous other costume roles and specializations. While those changes have been for the better, there is still a lot of work to do. Many people, and even some theatre professionals themselves, do not have a full understanding of the role of the costume designer and the costume team. The costume team, as well as the costumes, do not always get the credit and appreciation they deserve. Often costume professionals are still not paid as well as other roles within a production. This book will attempt to contribute to a better understanding of the field of costume and its communication. Furthermore, beyond the practical and functional content relating to costume and the costume designer, this book wants to open up the reader to the potential of the costume to have agency and the possibilities available to the costume practitioner.

APPROACH TO THE BOOK

This book is based on first-hand experience and numerous conversations with professionals from the theatre and film industries. The premise of this book is to represent these industries as they exist today and make information accessible to aspiring costume professionals, information that otherwise would not be as easily obtainable. It cannot be stressed enough, how many perspectives and approaches there exist within this field, which this book attempts to take into account. To remain compact and accessible, this book gives just enough detail to grasp the complexity of costume and the work of the costume designer. For the interested reader, there are many more books to read and more subjects to study. A list of further reading suggestions can be found at the end of this book.

While costume design can exist outside the boundaries of text, this book focuses on costume design for text-based theatre. Chapter 1, therefore, introduces methods to analyse a script and then seamlessly leads into an introduction to research methods. However, most methods and tools to which this book introduces the reader can be applied to performance that does not focus on text, such as dance, devised performance or experimental theatre. In fact, more concrete information about dance is given at various points in this book, as well as opera and film.

This book focuses on the various design methods, rather than one aspect of designing, such as drawing. While the basics of drawing and its role within design take up a lot of Chapter 2, there are plenty of alternative tools and methods available to the designer. This chapter, therefore, introduces the reader to the various other tools that the designer can apply when exploring and testing ideas. By doing so, this book intends to stress the explorative aspect to design and how vital it is in becoming a good designer. The understanding seems to be that designing costumes is the process of drawing a costume. However, a costume drawing is one of many tools to communicate a design and many designers choose to use other tools, such as draping, styling, collaging and writing, to communicate their ideas. How to do this effectively will be explored in Chapters 2 and 3.

No matter how good a designer is, understanding the performing arts' industry and operating effectively within it are vital for a designer's success. Chapters 5, 6 and 7 give an insight into the industry's structure and how a designer functions within it, while Chapter 7 goes into more detail on how to break into the industry and become a successful designer. Chapter 5 outlines the different roles available to a costume professional and, specifically, to the early career costume designer. It also goes into more depth with the various career pathways available to the designer; it outlines options available to the designer to support their practice. Furthermore, Chapter 7 points out practices that the designer can follow in order to become an established designer and to stay relevant.

The book is structured to reflect the design process from beginning to end. At the end of most chapters, the reader will find a number of exercises to test the knowledge gained and to build up skills. However, when going through the book and the exercises in sequence, a speculative design process could be followed based on a script of choice. Used in this way, this book offers aspiring designers the chance to conduct a speculative design project on their own terms, potentially resulting in great portfolio pieces.

THE FUNCTION OF THE COSTUME AND ITS CONTEXT

In most contexts, the function of costumes is to help tell a story: of the characters, in particular, and of the narrative of the script, in general. In many cases, a costume is successful when it does not draw a lot of attention; however, other productions allow for more flamboyant costumes. This book will go into great detail with the reasons for deciding for one or the other, and who the professionals are who make these decisions; it will come as no surprise that it is not the designer alone. Chapter 3 lists a variety of factors, referred to as parameters, such as the genre, form, style, venue, text and the creative team, that determine the direction of the costume design, often without the costume designer having even gotten involved. The creative team, of which the costume designer is an essential part, develops a concept for a production and decides on its form and style. Form and style, as well as the genre, are often already determined by the text or the company producing and staging it. The costume designer needs to be aware of this and the costumes need to appear in unison with the production to which they belong. They need to follow its logic.

The Different Industries, Genres and Forms

Costume design is a versatile profession and allows for a varied career. It is common to find designers working across dance, musicals, opera and theatre. Some costume designers design for musicians and some designers collaborate with professionals from the performance art scene. However, while many designers would like to work across various industries, it can be a challenge to carve out a career working across all the live performing arts, as well as film and TV.

In order to make the point that a career across various genres, industries and scenes is possible, this book covers the costume design process generally and emphasizes the overwhelming amount of overlap. There are fundamental aspects to design that are independent from whether designing costumes for film, theatre, dance or music. This book introduces design methods and tools that can be applied across the various industries, genres and forms. Methods to conduct research, to find inspiration and to develop a concept follow a similar protocol across the wide range of design disciplines. Before specializing, an aspiring designer is well advised to gain a good understanding of the fundamental design elements, which is what this book can offer.

However, different forms, such as film, opera and dance, for example, require specific knowledge, which will be pointed out throughout this book. In order to do so, the book gives additional information on dance, film and opera in several dedicated sections. By doing so, it intends to empower the aspiring designer to cross boundaries and embrace the similarities, while knowing the differences.

Beyond the information given in this book, the reader who is interested in any specific knowledge regarding designing costumes for film, opera, ballet or period, for example, is well advised to keep reading more specific books on the desired subject. A list of relevant and industry-approved books can be found at the end of this book.

Alternative Contexts

Increasingly, there is a development toward a cross-disciplinary approach to the performing arts. The boundaries of the various disciplines are being challenged and moved. Some costume practitioners concern themselves with a more experimental and investigative approach to costume and apply their work outside the context of traditional performance. Not every project needs to start with a job offer or be dependent on a fee. There are many different career set-ups available to the costume designer. One of them could be working within an art context and creating costumes outside the boundaries of a traditional performance.

New opportunities for costume designers and artists are emerging. The rise of animation films, for example, offers numerous new pathways for costume designers and who knows what the future holds. The role of the costume designer and the work attached to it are not set in stone and can, and should, always be further explored.

WHAT TO KEEP IN MIND BEFORE ACCEPTING A JOB OR GETTING INVOLVED IN A PROJECT

Before accepting a job offer, it is important that the designer has obtained all the necessary information, in order to assess whether a project will be worth their time and effort. These considerations should be of a financial nature, as well as with regard to their portfolio and reputation. Money plays a role, but whether or not a designer accepts a job is not merely dependent on that. A job might not generate the designer a lot of profit but might give them more exposure. A job might give the designer the chance to try something they have never tried before. A job might be a welcomed challenge that the designer might want at this point in their career. A job might get the designer useful press coverage because of the venue, the nature of the project or the collaborators. There are many considerations and questions for the costume designer, which the following section outlines briefly.

Collaboration

Being a costume designer is a highly collaborative profession. For a lot of professionals, that is the appeal. It is important to be aware of the everyday reality of working with people and being dependent on them in many different ways. To know what to expect from a project is vital. Before starting a project with another professional, or indeed accepting a job offer, it is useful to find out some information about them. There are many different ways of developing and creating a performance and approaching the designing of costume. The designer needs to make sure that a project is suitable for them.

When meeting a director, for example, it is important to gauge expectations and the degree of creative freedom a production will allow for. A director might demonstrate a great interest in period productions, which might or might not be of interest to the designer. There should be scope for negotiation, but often enough there is not. That might not always be up to the director, it might simply be the nature of the project that restricts the creative decision-making. More information on that can be found in Chapter 3 (Parameters and How to Navigate Them). Some designers are happy to work to the director's brief and a well-developed design idea; others, however, need a lot of creative freedom. It helps the director, the team and, actually, the designer themselves, to be clear about their preferences.

Nothing is worse than not voicing concerns in the beginning and then getting frustrated with a production and compromising it because of fundamental differences between the various creative people involved. Being clear and pushing for the best scenario while navigating hierarchies can be tricky and is certainly something a designer should, and will, learn over time. It is important for a designer to be aware of these different ways of working and to be realistic about whether a potential collaboration would be a fruitful match.

Challenges Concerning Experience, Diversity and Representation

Whether the designer feels that they are the right person for a production depends on their interests, style and work experience, as well as their confidence in themselves in being the right choice. What or who a designer represents and what their background is, could, and in some cases should, also play a role. The designer is advised to reflect on possible challenges before accepting a job offer or getting involved in a project. They might conclude that, for various reasons, they are the right choice. Equally, the designer or another member of the production team might not feel this way. Reasons for either of these views are multi-layered, and should be explored, discussed and reflected upon. It is good to keep in mind that concerns can always be challenged and, in many cases, should be challenged if the designer feels there are grounds to do so. Whatever the reason for the concern is, whether it has to do with experience, style, representation or diversity, any production benefits from a diverse and balanced team.

Money and Fees

While not every decision as to whether or not to get involved in a project should be dependent on money, a lot of the time it will be. Before accepting a job offer, the designer should find out the breakdown of fee, material and labour budget, and what will be expected of them. Ideally, there is a costume team calculated into the budget of a production and these individuals will have already been appointed, as would be the case when working for a large-scale opera or film. But often enough this is not the case and the costume designer will either have to find their team themselves or even take on other roles additionally to their role as designer. More detail on costume roles can be found in Chapter 5 (The Costume Team).

Workload

It is vital to find out exactly what the expectations for a role are, especially when they could extend beyond the costume design and into making,

sourcing, repair and maintenance. The designer might not have the interest in, experience for or means to meet the requirements of a particular role. On productions with bigger budgets, the costume designer will have a costume supervisor and access to a team of specialized makers. On smaller productions, it is not uncommon to expect a costume designer to partly or fully make or buy the costumes or engage makers, especially in dance. The amount of work involved in a production becomes particularly important when the designer is already busy.

Initial Questions

Answering the following questions will help a designer with the decision as to whether or not a job is suitable. Furthermore, they will determine all of the subsequent design steps; most importantly, the research required for a costume design. They should, therefore, be the starting point for any costume design.

- What is the context? Is it a play, opera, a dance piece, musical, performance art, film, TV-series, music video or an advertisement?
- Who is the director? What is their style?
- Which venue does it take place in? What kind of venue is it? What is its location?
- Who are the people involved?
- Does the director, choreographer or producer already have some ideas?
- Is there a brief?
- Was the costume designer approached because of their particular style?
- Is there a script? Is it devised?
- Is it new writing, a classic or an adaptation?
- What time period is it set in and should be set in?
- How much freedom is there for the costume designer to make it their own?
- How many characters are there and/or how many people have to be costumed?
- What is the budget?
- What is the timeline?

prominent use
of nature (flowers,
birds, ginko leaves,
peacock feathers)

AESTHETICISM

pink rose

nature

Cecily

Pre-Raphaelites ~ ROSSETTI

contrary

Algernon — dandy

{ less is more, sober and refined
hyper masculine
ethos of self-representation

London

simple perfection

Ebonised wood,
ebonised gilt furniture

DUALITY

countryside

underdress

Jack

serious

Augusta Bracknell — majestic

AESTHETICS & ETHICS

Oscar Wilde

satirical writing
=
comment on absurdity
of Victorian values

STRANGE DETAILS

FLAWS

Salomé
OSCAR WILDE
AUBREY BEARDSLEY
RAFAEL CANSINOS
ASSENS

caricature — distorts features
distorts lines
plays on scale
} Aubrey Beardsley

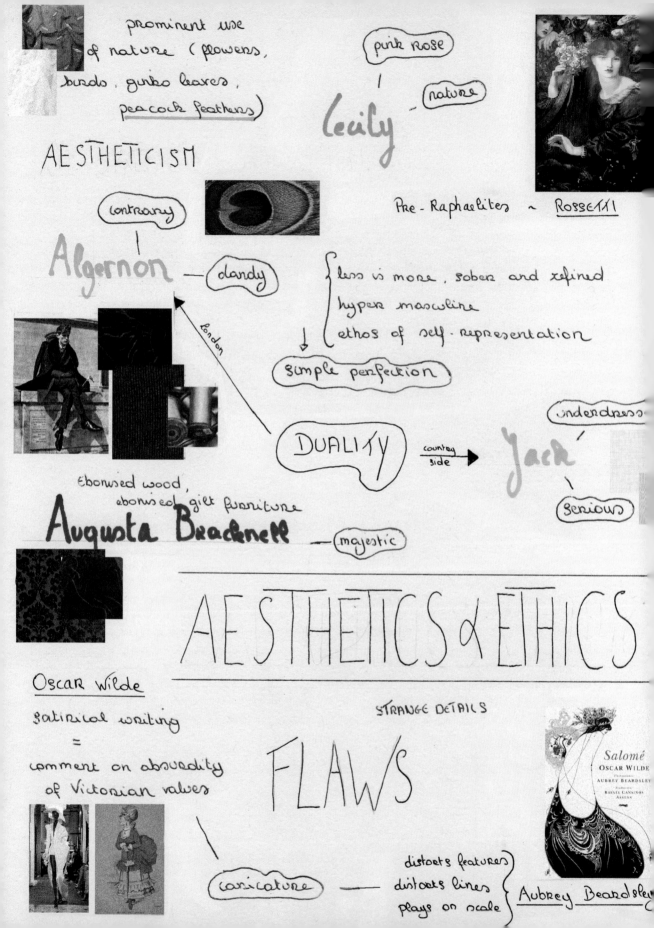

1
TEXT AND RESEARCH

It is of great significance to the design process whether or not a production starts with a text, also referred to as a script or play-text. Furthermore, whether the creative team follows the text precisely, or merely uses it as a jumping off point, impacts the design process tremendously. Some theatre-makers might use a text as a starting point to explore themes in it and others might adapt a play, a classic, for example, to fit a new circumstance. Whichever option is being pursued, most theatre productions, films and TV shows, opera productions and musicals use text. Broadly speaking, this book, and particularly this chapter, will focus on text-based productions and how to approach the reading and analysing of scripts. The tools to analyse a script introduced in the following paragraphs are suggestions and not necessarily used by every designer. Many designers follow them in some sort of variation, time permitting, but certainly other designers will have different approaches.

Non-text-based performance, on the other hand, is an equally significant field of interest for many performance-makers generally and costume designers in particular. For some performance-makers, the focus might be the delivering of a particular message or the exploration of the body, a costume, an object, a building, a theatre or a site and its particular history. That does not mean that text will not play an important role later in the process, but it means that their work is not text-centred or does not use text as a starting point. A performance that is not text-centred might start with a research and development phase, as opposed to analysing a script, and continues with the exploration of ideas or materials, which will be introduced in detail in Chapter 2. The designer might respond to situations arising during rehearsals, which is particularly common in devised and experimental theatre, as well as contemporary dance.

READING AND ANALYSING A SCRIPT

The aim of conducting research is not only finding more information, it is about being immersed in the world of the play. Sometimes that extends to the world of the playwright and the time and location the play is set in. Before reading a script, it might be advisable to find out whether there are any publications or playwright's introductory comments available. Furthermore, it will be useful to find out when the play was written and whether the script specifies a date or period in which it is set and where it is set. Some designers will also try and find out what the playwright's influences or their interests and motivations were. In the case of a newly written script, there might be the possibility to speak to the playwright directly. In most cases, when getting involved in a production of a new script, the playwright will be an essential part of the team with a great influence on the production. Before reading the script, it might be helpful to do brief research on it, the playwright and the time and place the script is set in. This will help to

OPPOSITE: Evelien Van Camp identifying themes and research subjects for *The Importance of Being Earnest* (1895, Oscar Wilde) created as part of the UAL Costume Design for Performance course, 2020. Organizing information visually can be helpful in understanding it, giving it more structure and remembering it.

easier understand the script when reading through it. In the case of *The Importance of Being Earnest*, for example, a play written by Oscar Wilde in 1895, it will be inevitable to learn more about Oscar Wilde, his life and the time he was living in when trying to gain an understanding of the script. It seems significant to know that he was married to a woman, yet had a male lover. His double-life shows obvious parallels to the protagonist in the play. The knowledge about Wilde having had to deny his homosexuality, as it was strictly unlawful to engage in a romantic relationship with a person of the same sex, opens up the text to a deeper understanding.

Looking at social, political and artistic developments of the time a script is set in, will further its understanding. Oscar Wilde participated in the trend of being a dandy and was a part of the aesthetic movement. This knowledge not only helps with the interpretation of the text, but also with finding inspiration and a design approach. *A Streetcar Named Desire*, a play written by Tennessee Williams in 1951, centres around a woman with a particularly fragile mental state, who visibly deteriorates over the course of the play. It might be useful to know that Williams' own sister was diagnosed with schizophrenia a few years before he finished this script. Whether or not that gives any more insight into the play and, furthermore, can inform the costume, cannot always be measured in a direct way, but it gives the designer a deeper understanding of the context of the script. What is important for the designer is to have a full understanding of the text, its context and its world.

The First Read-Through

The first read-through will become more useful, and possibly even more enjoyable, when the designer has researched the main facts about the script beforehand. However, some designers might want to just read it and let the message and its 'feel' naturally emerge, rather than diving right into an analysis. Other designers might start analysing the script immediately and want to find

Research and costume design ideas by Jody Broom for Blanche of *A Streetcar Named Desire* (1951, Tennessee Williams), created as part of the UAL Costume Design for Performance course, 2020.

as much information about it as possible. While this might be a matter of preference, other factors like time might require a designer to start analysing it straight away. It is common for a designer to read a script to determine if they want to get involved in the production. In this scenario, they would not invest any more work into it other than a quick read through. In the case of a classic text, for example, it is likely that the designer is already familiar with the material and starts their process by working through the text already in more detail. Either way, the designer will have to read through the text several times at several stages over the course of the production period. When working on a theatre production, the designer will likely be invited to a 'read-through' at the beginning of rehearsals. While this gives the designer the chance to hear the words and see the actors, it is often too late in the process to have an influence on the design. The designer should try to imagine the scenes and how they could appear on stage. This will help them to gain a better understanding of the story and the potential of the design.

Initial Questions When Reading Through a Script

CHARACTERS
- How many characters are there?
- Who are they and how do they relate to each other?
- Where do the characters come from and where are they going?
- Are there any costume changes?
- What does the play indicate that the characters might wear? Is anything specifically mentioned?
- Who is in each scene and where do they enter and exit from?
- Can some characters form groups?
- Is there an ensemble? Do they sing/dance? How many of them are there?

There will often be a character list at the beginning of the script, stating the character names and, in some cases, the age, relationship to other characters and their social position.

LOCATION
- What are the different locations?

This includes countries and regions, cities, landscapes, whether it plays indoors or outdoors, possibly the type of house, rooms or something more abstract or undefined, e.g. 'a frightening place'.

TIME
- What is the year, month, day, season and time of the day in which the play and its various scenes are set?
- Is there a significant jump in time somewhere in the play?
- Is the play going back in time or jumping backwards and forwards?
- Is there a change in period?

Making sense of time is crucial to understanding the journey a character takes and the costumes they will wear throughout.

UNDERSTANDING DRAMATIC STRUCTURE ACTS/SCENES AND UNITS
- How many scenes and acts does the script have, what happens in them and who appears in them?

A play, opera or musical is made up of a number of scenes. These scenes are grouped into acts, which structure the narrative development. Scenes contain a group of characters in a particular location in a moment in time. A scene change is when the location or players on stage shift. Sometimes, the playwright does not use scenes and acts to structure the script. In this case, the designer and director need to break the script down into scenes themselves in order to ease the design process. Furthermore, the designer might want to further break down the scenes, into so-called units, to indicate a change in direction of a scene, such as its energy, mood, purpose or tone, for example.

STAGE DIRECTIONS

- Are there stage directions and, if so, do they need to be followed?

Stage directions are comments made by the playwright about the characters, setting or atmosphere, for example, but their purpose can vary widely. They can give the reader more information on what has happened or is happening in a particular scene, for example. They are not part of the script. They can help the reader to understand the playwright's intent or they can be about the staging or technical aspects. They are a useful reference, but they do not need to be followed entirely, unless otherwise stated in the designer's contract, by the playwright or, indeed, if the director insists and there is no ground for negotiation.

MOOD AND ATMOSPHERE

- What is the mood and atmosphere of the play or individual scenes?

They are often commented on in dialogue or described in the stage directions, for example, comments about the weather or quality of light.

A FEW MORE QUESTIONS

- What season is it and does this change?
- What time is it and how much time passes from the beginning to the end of the play?
- Is there any symbolism in the play?
- What are the overall themes?
- What is the message?
- What is the essence of the play?

These are complex questions, and they will not all be answered after the first read-through. It might take a few readings and conversations; for example, with the director or even the writer, if that is an option. However, it is important not to lose sight of these questions and to keep trying to answer them. A significant part of designing is being organized and disciplined. Logical thinking and thinking ideas through are essential.

Tools to Analyse a Script

Whatever the approach to analysing a script might be, applying a method will significantly help structuring the answers to the above questions and any thoughts resulting from them. While every designer develops their own unique design approach, there are a number of tools used by designers in some sort of variation, even if they are not fully aware of it. The following sections introduce the reader to the most common ones.

THE SCENE BREAKDOWN

Conducting a scene breakdown is the most time-consuming of all the tools, but it is also the most useful first step in the design process for a play or film. The designer will go through the script and note down all necessary information, as well as their own thoughts, in relation to their findings. Many scripts are already divided into acts and scenes, which is a good starting point for the designer to structure their script breakdown. For various reasons, the designer can further break down the script into units. That would be an individual choice and concerns mostly design considerations, such as costume changes, character appearances, props requirements, set configuration, video projections and changes in lighting, music, mood and atmosphere. The best approach to organize this information is to insert it into a chart, rather than just using a list. The information collated in this chart can be actual facts from the script, their interpretations by the designer, as well as their notes and thoughts. The aim of the chart is not necessarily to get all the facts right, it is first and foremost to understand the play and how it unfolds scene by scene. This is not a document that needs to be shared with the director, although it will greatly help conversations with the creative team.

SCENES ACTS UNITS	CHARACTERS PRESENT	DESCRIPTION	DAY TIME YEAR	LOCATION	COSTUME	PROPS	SET	LIGHT MOOD
1/1	Fiorello Count Almaviva A band of musicians	All gather near the house Rosina lives in, all play music and sing all day until the disappointed count Almaviva dismisses everybody	Early 18th century Early morning, before sunrise until evening	A square in Seville, a Spanish town	Count wears a cloak		Bartolo's house	Sunset Dim light Moody
1/1/2	Count Figaro	Figaro introduces himself in famous cavatina (song) while the count is hiding. Pretty long solo	Dawn	Same square		What is the chorus doing while singing? Are they using any props?		
1/1/3	Count Figaro Later briefly Bartolo (leaving his house) Rosina visible from behind the window	Figaro gives the Count more information on Rosina Bartolo leaves The count sings for Rosina who responds to it The count pretends to be somebody else named Lindoro		In front of Figaro's shop on a square Front of Bartolo's house, possibly with a door	Bartolo dressed up for town Count is dressed up as 'Lindoro'		Count: "I watch near this balcony" Figaro: 'the balcony window opens'	
1/1/4	Count Figaro	Long duet in which they make a plan. Figaro suggests for the count to disguise as a soldier and pretend to be drunk looking for shelter in Bartolo's house.	Evening/ Night	Same location as above		Figaro sings about gold (could be interesting visually)	Figaro's shop: number 15, white front, 'pomade divine' Five wigs in the window, a sign, four steps, a lantern	Dim night light, conspira-torial
1/2	Rosina Figaro	Rosina's cavatina in which she introduces herself. Conversation between Figaro and Rosina. Promise to meet again to talk about something.	Possibly in the middle of the day.	On Bartolo's premises (a courtyard of some sort)		Rosina holds a letter in her hand	"I'm living inside a sepulchre." They can hear/see Bartolo coming home. Figaro hides and then disappears.	Bright light sunshine outside. Dimly lit in the house

This chart is an example of a scene breakdown using the opera *The Barber of Seville* (1816, Rossini). It is not meant to be exhaustive but to give an idea of how a scene breakdown could be approached.

MAPPING THE APPEARANCE OF CHARACTERS THROUGHOUT A PLAY

It can be very helpful to know how many performers there are on stage at one particular time in the play and the general flow of people coming on and leaving the stage throughout the play. The work of the designer becomes particularly interesting and relevant when characters appear together on stage and consequently form an image. The more characters there are on stage, the more visible the design concept will become. This is the moment when characters are seen in relation to each other, and colours and shapes often grow in importance. This is where costume design gets more complex, but it is also the moment when the costume designer can shine. The best way to make sense

Act 1 Scene	Earnest (John Worthing)	Algernon	Gwendolen	Lady Bracknell	Cecily	Miss Prism	Reverend Chasuble
1							
2							
3							
4							
5							
6							
7							
8							

Act 2 Scene	Earnest (John Worthing)	Algernon	Gwendolen	Lady Bracknell	Cecily	Miss Prism	Reverend Chasuble
1							
2							
3							
4							
5							
6							
7							
8							
9							

Act 3 Scene	Earnest (John Worthing)	Algernon	Gwendolen	Lady Bracknell	Cecily	Miss Prism	Reverend Chasuble
1							
2							
3							

Mapping out the movement of characters can be very helpful for understanding the flow of the play or to determine whether costume changes will work. This chart is an example using Oscar Wilde's *The Importance of Being Earnest* (1895). To allow for a clearer picture, the script was divided into scenes as well as acts, although Wilde used only acts to structure his play. To see the flow of characters coming on and off the stage, it can be helpful to use a different colour for each character.

of the characters' movements is to make it visual, in a chart, for example, and by colour-coding each character.

CHARACTER'S QUOTATIONS CHART

A helpful way to find out more about the characters is to gather what characters say about each other in the script and note it down. An effective visual solution to this might be to draw up a chart that lists all characters in the first column and again across the first line. The first column indicates the quoted characters, and the first line indicates the characters whom they talk about. It becomes clearer when looking at the example.

What Character A says about B	Skilling	Lay	Fastow	Roe	Raptors (abstract characters that symbolize the fake companies Enron created to hide debt)
Skilling	Act I, Scene 3: my father was a valve salesman. I,5: I'm fucking smart. I,9: all these ideas are mine. II,3: I went to Harvard. II,7: I haven't killed anyone. III,5: I believe I am innocent. III,6: It means it's just me.	I,2: doesn't get me. I didn't grow up on a farm. I,3: your daddy was a Baptist church. I,7: the smartest or the dumbest motherfucker in the world. II,2: got to accept it's my show	I,1: this guy gets it. I,5: that's cos you're weak. I,8: you've saved my fucking life. I,9: not a performer got his own qualities. He's mine II, 8: I created you	I,1 : may've seen her in vogue. I,3: You're a politician. I don't want to work for you. I,9: she is jealous. Everything is the Claudia Roe Show.	II,1 : What the fuck is this. II,8: we're getting rid of them.
Lay	(to Roe) He could learn something from you in charm. I,5: golden boy	I,3: I believe in god, democracy and the company. I'm as old as plains. II,10 : I am a safe pair of hand	I,9: He is hardly the life and soul. Roe thinks we should keep an eye on him III,9: you don't belong to me boy.	I,1 : Our star abroad I,3: you were always my favourite. I,9: it's a very. entertaining show II,2: Didn't show a lot of class.	
Fastow	I,1: I,5: I won't let you down. I,8: who's done more for me in this world	I,1: He's just a guy	I,4: remember that when I'm CFO III, 3: I believed I was a hero. I was extremely greedy which I regret.	I,1 : You can't get Lay away from Claws. It's like she is a carer	I,8: like in Jurassic park I,9: clever girls II, 1 : these sort of entities. II,8: it's sick II,9: I'm sorry girls
Roe	I,2 Look at your face. You just changed. You're a real son of a ...You're a godless atheist I,3 : doesn't have skills to manage people. Got trouble relating to others. He doesn't remember names. I,7: you look good. You went to that college in Pennsylvania	II,3: had faith in me.	I,7: your guy with the suit and the hair.	I,7: I'm fighting to survive here.	
Trader	I,4: There is nothing Skilling don't know.		I,4: Lapdog motherfucker. Douche breasted douchebag, thinks he is Sinatra		
Raptors					
Lawyer	II,7: You are getting the bad press.	Ken Lay died.			
Analyst	II,9: The big JS is losing it here.				

Example of a character's quotations' chart using the play *Enron* (2009, Lucy Prebble). Characters talk about each other and while this is not always truthful, it still reveals something about both characters, the one who said it and the one who was talked about. References to clothing are of particular interest but other information that helps to develop a character should also be paid attention to.

Understanding Themes and Motifs Through Vocabulary

Words, and playing with them, can be a great tool to develop design ideas. While reading through a script, most designers make notes, for example, of words that are key to an understanding or interpretation of the text, that stand out or have a particular association, maybe with a certain colour or shape. It might be a word that is repeated a lot or that conjures up a certain feeling. The words noted down might be taken directly from the text or might already be a response to the text. They can be valid for the whole play or for a particular act, scene or unit. After having found a few words, the designer could play with them, for example, by combining them, perhaps into unusual pairs. Of particular interest could be combinations of words that stimulate the creative mind, for example, words that result in a contradiction, exaggeration, a deeper meaning or subversion.

There are an almost infinite number of words and combinations from which the designer could choose. The tables offer a starting point.

Colour	Shape	Value
Vivid	Close	Dark
Washed-out	Angular	Medium
Cool	Regular	Light
Earthy	Irregular	Harsh
Neutral	Sharp	Intense
Loud	Graceful	Sombre
Monochrome	Chunky	Bleached

Texture	Line	Space
Rough	Angular	Spacious
Soft	Soft	Foreground
Hard	Free	Negative
Smooth	Strong	Positive
Lush	Broken	Airy
Shiny	Fluid	Confined
Dense	Long	Claustrophobic

Sarah Bottomley responding with a selection of relevant words to her first read-through of the script *A Streetcar named Desire* (1951, Tennessee Williams), created as part of the UAL Costume Design for Performance course, July 2020.

LAUNCHPAD IDEAS

After reading through the text, the designer, together with the director perhaps, might be well advised to clarify or, indeed, identify the main themes on which they want to focus. Taking these as the starting point, and the vocabularies found through the tool above, they can play around with words to develop phrases. These phrases could function as a launchpad from which to develop design ideas. They might change over the course of the production and after conversations with the rest of the creative team, but they will help with developing design ideas. There could also be different launchpad ideas for different scenes.

Every creative team will identify their own themes and approach these in their own way, resulting in unique design solutions. The examples provided in this table are, therefore, merely a demonstration of the tool and by no means universally true. The choice of plays attempts to include in particular classics from a variety of periods and of various styles, forms and genres, as they are widely known and performed. A speculative design for a classic text is a useful addition to a portfolio, as it will be more likely to mean something to the onlooker. However, reading and watching modern plays and new writing by well-known and emerging playwrights is highly recommended.

Play	Some identified subjects	Examples of launchpad ideas
Enron by Lucy Prebble (2009, early 2000s USA)	Greed, betrayal, instrumentalization of people and the mass	Harsh humanity
Sing Yer Hearts out for the Lads by Roy Williams (2002, early 2000s Leeds, England)	Race, class, UK politics, football, tribalism, passion	Raw realism
Blasted by Sarah Kane (1995, 1990s England)	Violence against women, war, the personal is political, time/change, brutality, survival, love	Subtle violence
A Streetcar named Desire by Tennessee Williams (1951, 1950s New Orleans, USA)	Mental health, social status, family history	Beautiful decay
Threepenny Opera by Berthold Brecht (1928, set in Victorian London, England)	Power struggle, greed, corruption, capitalism, irony, selfishness	Fragile power
The Importance of Being Earnest by Oscar Wilde (1895, Edwardian England)	Deception, masculinity, image, class, beauty, sex, marriage economy, Victorian society	Ridiculously perfect
Alice in Wonderland by Lewis Carroll (1865, Victorian England, a play based on the famous novel)	Lost innocence, coming of age, identity, drugs, multiple realities, home	Dissonant magic
Rheingold by Richard Wagner (1850, opera with mythological setting)	Greed, rejection, debts, revenge, territory, theft	Weathered dreams
The Barber of Seville by Rossini (1816, opera set in Seville, Spain)	Forbidden love, disguise, loyalty	Stained vulnerability

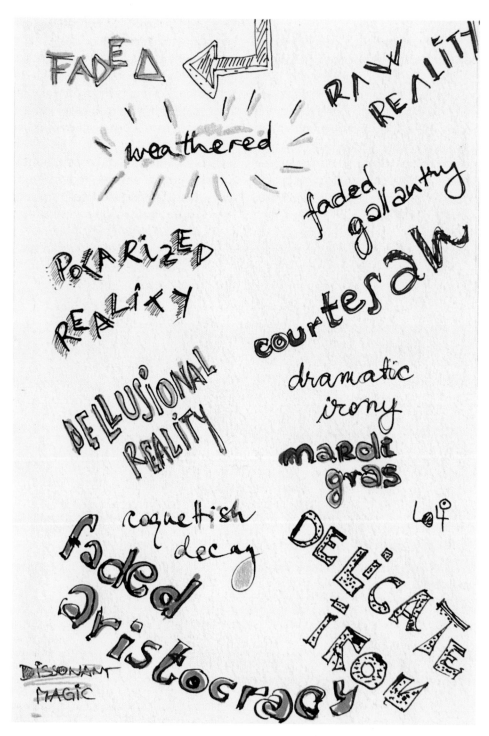

Viola Borsos developing ideas for *A Streetcar named Desire* (1951, Tennessee Williams), as part of the UAL Costume Design for Performance course, 2020. Creating a visually interesting mind-map is not only enjoyable, but it allows for further immersion into a world. Similar to doodling, this form of searching for ideas can help to feel less pressured, while allowing working in a more intuitive way.

RESEARCH

The Importance of Research

Conducting research about a play and subject matter is one of the most important tasks in the costume design process. A profound knowledge of the play, the playwright, the context of the play, the political and social climate, as well as the key subject matter, is vital when developing a design concept. Without this fundamental knowledge, the design is subject to incoherence, triviality and an indulgence in a particular aesthetic without a deeper meaning or connection to the text and the playwright's intention. The designer will be conducting research throughout the design process but there will be a point, mostly before starting to explore ideas further, when the bulk of the research will be concluded.

There are many approaches to research and with the internet and new forms of technology it is an ever-changing practice. How the designer

A pin-wall with reference images collected from books and online sources combined with costume drawings and sketches by Ysa Abba Dora for Oscar Wilde's *The Importance of Being Earnest* (1895), created as part of the UAL Costume Design for Performance short course, 2019.

conducts their research is very much dependent on the individual project, the designer's preferences, their team, the director, the circumstances, the period and subject matter. Research can take many forms and does not always mean going to a library or searching endlessly through webpages. Some designers cannot get enough of reading and looking through books and images; for others, however, this might not lead to the desired surge of inspiration and enthusiasm. Should this be the case, the designer needs to find other ways to conduct their research. It is important to feel connected to the subject matter and to be fully immersed in the world of the play in order to develop great ideas and begin to piece together the feel of its visual representation.

Conducting research could take the designer to a location significant to the play or talking to people that might give them more insights. Research could bring the designer to a museum or an art exhibition. It could take them to another town, city or even country, or to a cafe to observe people. It could prompt the designer to attend a church service or to visit a mosque. The necessity to talk to a particular community and to find out about their customs could arise. After having obtained a good general idea of the play and its context, the main focus of the research will be getting to know the play's characters really well.

When making discoveries about other cultures, it is important to be mindful of how this information is used and how it informs the design. In recent years there has been a rise in awareness that simply taking an inspiration from other cultures, such as a costume detail, and working it into a design could be controversial and received with mixed feelings by the respective people of that culture. There needs to be a conversation around how to represent other cultures. Closely linked with this awareness is the need for the creative team to understand how their own background influences their design instincts. Most projects require the team to educate themselves about aspects of the subject matter and themes present in the script, which is why the research phase is so important.

The Research List

In order to contain and direct their research, the designer needs to identify keywords and topics before commencing their work. The best way to approach this is free-associating any knowledge, words and phrases, themes and questions about the text and organize this into a list, 'the research list'. This list will then help the search in an online library catalogue, an online seller such as Amazon or search engines such as Google. Keywords need to be useful, precise and specific. General phrases such as 'Victorian dress' will bring hundreds of results, whereas a more specific one such as 'Victorian working-class in London' or 'children's clothes in Victorian England' might narrow down the search. While internet search engines, such as Google, will attempt to correct spelling mistakes and offer suggestions, a library catalogue is, currently, not as flexible when it comes to spelling mistakes and a lack of useful keywords. A quick search on Wikipedia will help to obtain basic knowledge and simple facts to get the research list started. The online encyclopaedia is a platform that has been equally praised and criticized, but it is simply unbeatable in obtaining basic information very quickly. Further research will have to be conducted to determine what is correct, what to discard and what is worth pursuing. When needing to find reliable information and to confirm facts, the designer will have to resort to books, newspapers, journals, published essays and articles or academic papers. The reader can find a selection of resources in the further reading list in the Appendix.

Answering the following questions is a good starting point for a research list:

• Who is the playwright?
• Where is the playwright from?
• Is the playwright alive? When did the playwright live?
• What is/was the era of the playwright? In which context did the playwright write the book?
• What is/was the social and political background when the play was written?

- Is/was the playwright part of any art, literary, political or philosophical movement?
- Who are/were the playwright's friends?
- Who are/were the contemporaries of the playwright: the key thinkers, artists, painters, commentators, illustrators, photographers, architects and philosophers?
- What are the main themes of the play? (This question is much more complex and, therefore, will take a while to answer but should be considered right from the beginning.)

Once a script-specific research list has been established, the words and themes can be used to search the internet, catalogues, social media platforms, Amazon and Pinterest to find imagery, books, articles and even relevant events and places to visit. Last but not least, it will be useful to look at how the themes of a play have influenced other artists and architects.

How to Look

Whether researching online or in a library, it is important to find images and information from different sources. Images of the fashion of a particular period, for example, should be a selection of photographs of people of the time, illustrations, fashion plates, caricatures, etchings, paintings, political cartoons and photographs of fashion collections. To fully understand a piece of clothing, it is important to also find images of clothing in motion. Libraries with a good fashion and costume collection will offer great books on uniforms and workwear worth studying. The reader can find a list of libraries and online image archives in the Appendix. Depending on the period the play is set in, a designer might be able to visit costume collections, relevant locations, exhibitions or events to collect imagery and information relevant to their production. It is important to search beyond fashion plates and photographs of costumes and study the culture of a particular country and its customs, to look at architecture, interior design, sculpture, textile, furniture-making and painting, for example.

When searching for costume references of a particular period, the designer needs to also look for imagery of people that actually lived at the time. Personalities of a specific period represent the fashion of the time more realistically. Depending on the period of the play, those might be restricted to members of the Royal family of the region, key thinkers of the time, celebrities, dancers, actors, artists, politicians and scientists.

This is because other members of society presented little reason to be painted or photographed. More recent periods might allow the designer to find a broader variety of people; however, this can still be a challenge. People tend to have their pictures taken and publicize them for specific reasons only – that reason is the key to finding them. Watching films or TV series and looking through magazines, newspapers and social media accounts might produce useful results. Similarly to a fashion exhibition, vintage shops allow the designer to study clothing in more depth, which is another research option. Most second-hand shops will have a selection from the last few fashion decades, as people often hold on to certain items of clothing for years before giving them away. Fashion plates, on the other hand, only show the ideal way of dressing, often only adopted by the trendiest people of the time and those that were able to afford it.

While it is a lot easier to grasp an aesthetic with the benefit of hindsight, it tends to be a bit more challenging to make sense of the current society and its fashion. Available information is not yet as organized and filtered. For that reason, the designer needs to be a bit more inventive and investigative. More current sources will need to be used, such as social media, blogs and websites that centre around people and clothing. Visiting relevant places and observing its visitors or inhabitants can become a necessary task. Depending on which place this is, for example, a prison or school, being granted access and finding ways to document observations might require a little extra work. However, observing people in public places and cafes, for example, should be an easy and enjoyable activity, as long as it is relevant to the design.

It is important to be aware of the fact that not all people who can afford the latest fashion will actually adopt it. That is true today as much as it was true a hundred years ago. Especially in the case of older characters, the designer has to consider dressing them in the fashion from when they were younger, which might even be a decade prior to the time the play is set in. An older, well-to-do lady in an English play set around the 1890s, for example, might still hold on to the Victorian way of dressing, as this would have been the time she grew up in and developed her style and taste. A younger woman in the same play, on the other hand, might have adopted the most up-to-date fashion of the time, the Edwardian dress. It could well be that this young woman spends all her money on extravagant clothes and considers this a worthwhile investment, while actually not having much money at all. Another young woman might have the means to adopt the latest fashion but chooses not to and instead has developed a much more pared-down version of it. A working-class woman in the same play, however, will most likely not be able to think much about fashion at all and would wear a functional dress, regardless of her age. These principles can be applied to any period.

It is extremely important to always make a note of the source and author of a reference, especially when used in a mood board or presentation. This will not only ensure that it can always be found again but also gives credit to other professionals' work, besides abiding by copyright rules.

Where to Look

Books

Using books, as opposed to using the internet, to conduct research is still relevant to most designers, even though a library visit or a book purchase has become more of a special occasion to many. With increasingly more time spent in front of a screen, it might be the case that designers will embrace the use of books as a well-deserved break from the screen and vast online world. Furthermore, it can

The beginning of a production is dominated by conducting research and looking through hundreds of images. It is a period for asking relevant questions and making discoveries that spark the designer's imagination.

be a tedious task to look through hundreds of web-pages and thousands of images. Online sources can be misleading and crediting incorrect or simply absent, making it a time-consuming endeavour, which is especially challenging when time is of the essence. Books, on the other hand, have to go through a rigorous process of editing and fact-checking, resulting in a well-organized and coherent presentation of information that is relevant to its context. Many designers decide to try and build up their own personal library at their studio or home. Some designers, who are in the financial position to do so, attempt to purchase a couple of books during each production they are working on to slowly build up this library. If costs are a challenge, and for many other good reasons, it might be worth building up a digital reference library as well and work on it whenever there is a little bit of time to spare. Sources could be books found in libraries or trusted sources online, such as image archives of museums additionally to the Internet in general. A selection of those can be found in the Appendix. It would be misleading to remain quiet about just how much the internet has changed the process of researching. Designers can now save time by finding most information online, which certainly challenges the use of the book and questions its form going forward. However, it might not replace the book entirely, and poses many new challenges, as laid out below.

ONLINE

The internet has revolutionized research by making it a lot simpler and quicker to find relevant images that in the past would have taken a designer a long time to find and access. When designing a specific period dress, for example, the designer just needs to type in relevant keywords and consequently will be presented with an infinite number of images. However, while this is the most astonishing tool, using the internet does not necessarily simplify the research. On the contrary, it can indeed make it a lot more complicated and overwhelming at times. It is, therefore, advisable to develop methods, such as the research list mentioned earlier in this chapter, and follow them. Anybody who has conducted a Google search without a suitable set of keywords will have experienced frustration to some degree. Whether searching with Google,

in a library online catalogue, on Amazon or Ebay, having the right search terms is crucial. As laid out above, it is vital to take enough time and care when creating a good research list.

In the last few years, online catalogues have become the norm for pretty much any library, which means that searching through libraries can be done remotely and mostly without a library membership. Their interfaces are steadily improving from the often rather cumbersome navigation process they used to present their visitors with in the past. Furthermore, libraries, museums and specialist research centres increasingly offer access to a vast number of electronic resources and online image archives. Online image archives are very different from looking through images on a Google search or Pinterest. Image archives of museums, for example, are well researched and presented, credited correctly and organized into years and/or subjects. It is possible to find a lot more relevant images in a dedicated archive than when doing the much less specific Google search. In a Google search, any kind of image from any source can come up; and often images are credited wrongly. The findings on Google can be very helpful but can equally turn out to be quite frustrating, even misleading.

While design research relies heavily on images, it needs to be pointed out that images alone might not be sufficient to gain a deep enough understanding of a script and its subject matter. Conducting research will also have to include reading about a subject matter, about cultures, their customs and about specific garments and costumes. The internet increasingly offers dedicated research platforms where electronic versions of books, essays and other academic papers can be accessed, either free of charge or for a subscription fee.

LIBRARIES AND LIBRARY CATALOGUES

The function of libraries is undeniably changing, most significantly the shift to electronic resources. Before getting into more detail about the ever-growing online services, it needs to be said that they do not always make a library visit obsolete. Besides those designers preferring to hold a book in their hands, most libraries offer other types of resources such as special collections, sheet-music, objects, games or toys. Very often, when being a member, items can be reserved online to be picked up or looked at later and renewed online. Libraries can be useful in other ways. They offer an alternative workspace, for example, a space to conduct focused and specialist research. It is a place to connect to other people, possibly peers. The library functions as a community hub and society might see a renewed need for such a space.

Beyond its local function, library websites increasingly function as an entry point to conduct academic research and connect the researcher with other relevant websites. Library catalogues are accessible from any computer with internet access, which means the designer can conduct preliminary research online before deciding which library to visit or book to purchase. It has gradually become common practice to access electronic resources through library websites. Finding an electronic version of a script, for example, is useful, or an essay about a playwright, dissertations on relevant subject matter, films, documentaries and, of course, electronic versions of books. Furthermore, most libraries offer to browse a shelf, giving the visitor the chance to see alternative or similar books to the book of interest. The online presence of libraries opens up possibilities to look through libraries that are far away from the designer's location and to access their electronic resources. A London-based designer, for example, could be looking for information on American history in one of the various great libraries across the USA. The Appendix offers a small list of a few significant libraries across the world. This list does not attempt to be exhaustive but offers the reader a starting point for their online research.

SPECIALIST LIBRARIES

Specialist libraries offer a selection of books and many other resources that are specific to its focus, such as American history, prehistoric history, maritime life, art, architecture, anthropology and much more. These libraries can be particularly helpful when challenged by insufficient search results online or the limited and general content of regular libraries. There is a vast number of specialist libraries around the world and most of them can be accessed online. Some offer a great number of electronic resources too; others are restricted to actual visits. They function as hubs for their respective research focus and facilitate connecting individuals to other resources. A lot of specialist libraries are attached to research centres.

Their image archives offer access to well-researched and documented, often rare, collections of photographs and documents, and can simply be found on the library's website. However, navigating through a library website can be more difficult than finding the direct link to the image archive through a search engine such as Google. Some libraries make access very simple, while others require a membership or subscription. A lot of specialist libraries are reference-only libraries, which means that visitors can only look at books, rather than borrow them. Making copies or taking photographs is rarely a problem. A list of specialist libraries and image archives can also be found in the Appendix.

OTHER SOURCES

Costume and Fashion Museums and Collections
It is highly likely that looking exclusively at books and images will not satisfy the designer, and other ways to find information and inspiration will need to be pursued. For example, at some point in the research process it might become necessary to look at examples of period costume up close and not just a photograph. The designer might, therefore, visit a costume museum, a costume archive or a costume-hire place. Museums such as The Victoria and Albert Museum in London and the Fashion Museum in Bath collect and display great examples of eighteenth- and nineteenth-century fashion. Other countries, regions and towns will have their own version of a costume museum, and a simple online search will most certainly assist in finding them. For twentieth-century fashion, it might be worth looking at fashion houses and designers of the period, such as Chanel and Dior. Many fashion houses have accessible costume collections and travelling

exhibitions that come to all major museums around the world. The following examples can only give an inkling of how many collections there are:

- Musée Yves Saint Laurent, Paris
- Bata Shoe Museum, Toronto, Canada
- Kyoto Costume Institute, Kyoto, Japan
- Christian Dior Museum and Garden, Granville, France
- Cristóbal Balenciaga Museoa, Getaria, Spain
- Costume Institute at the Metropolitan Museum of Art, New York, USA
- Victoria and Albert Museum, London, UK
- Gucci Garden, Florence, Italy

The Victoria and Albert Museum, for example, has created exhibitions displaying the work of designers such as Dior, Balenciaga, Chanel, Vivienne Westwood and Alexander McQueen, which have travelled to other museums around the world. It is well possible that a relevant temporary exhibition or display is showing in a place nearby at a time when it seems like a good idea to search beyond the book and screen. Such exhibitions are a spectacle and often a great opportunity to see unique garments up close. It is, therefore, important to make the most of it and study the garments on display,

maybe in the form of sketching and, if possible, taking pictures, especially of interesting and unusual details. An exhibition does not always have to be relevant to the subject matter or even the period of interest. It can simply be an inspiring experience.

Costume-Hire Companies
Costume-hire companies are places of great importance to the theatre and film industry. They employ, in many cases, hundreds of costume professionals that care for thousands of well-organized and well-maintained costumes of all periods. Beyond that, they offer many other services, such as making costumes, supervising on productions or assisting designers. Not only are these places an incredible resource in which to find costumes or get them manufactured, they can also offer great inspiration and an opportunity to study costume. However, they do not operate like a museum or exhibition, where anybody

This picture shows the costume store of the English National Opera in London. The designer working on a production for the ENO will have the luxury of access to thousands of costume items. This can make the realization process of the costumes not only a lot easier, but also a lot more environmentally friendly when re-using costumes, rather than buying brand new clothes.

with a ticket can come in. They only allow access under particular conditions, such as the request of a service. A lot of designers will have built up a good relationship with their trusted costume-hire place and are granted invaluable access to endless information and inspiration. Europe has a few major costume-hire places in its biggest cities, such as London and Madrid, for example, and so has the USA in places such as New York City or Los Angeles. Versions of these will be found across the globe and can certainly be tracked down with a little bit of research and investigation. A list of companies can be found in the Appendix. A little side note: these companies offer a wider range of career paths for costume professionals and can be a great entry point into the industry.

Film, Television and Real Life
Sometimes the focus needs to shift from solely looking at images of clothing, fashion and costume, to looking at clothing in context, such as films, events, schools, prisons or fun fairs. A visit to a city, a street or a cafe to look at people and their context might be very helpful and equally inspiring. Watching films and television of a particular period, or indeed current productions, can be a fantastic source of inspiration and references. However, it is important to keep in mind, that the depiction of a specific period might not be entirely accurate and that findings need to be double-checked.

Social Media and Private Sources
Social media can be a very helpful tool in finding images, as well as individuals that are experts on particular aspects of costume design and costume-making or who have a special costume collection. Facebook offers a wide range of groups for costume professionals focusing on designers, makers or services, for example, or on industries such as television, film or theatre. Some unions or clubs have a representation on Facebook or other social media that would be worth joining or following. Instagram has various accounts dedicated to costume research and/or costume-making.

HOW TO GET STARTED DESIGNING COSTUMES

Exploring Ideas

One of the most challenging moments for a lot of aspiring designers and professionals alike is in fact stopping the research and beginning to explore

Research needs to lead into a phase of exploring ideas. Working some of that research into a collage is an effective tool for exploring ideas.

ideas. Perhaps the reason for this is that the focus is not so much on exploring ideas but that instead a lot of pressure is placed on having all the answers. A reason could be the presumption that the next step in the design process is drawing fully formed costume ideas on to perfect figurines. However, this commences at a much later point on the design timeline, after ideas have been fully explored. Exploring ideas is not only one of the most important parts of designing costumes but also the step that is often missed out when talking about designing. Making collages, sketching, draping, styling, writing and generally playing are ways of processing ideas that are very different from researching, reading and choosing the right image. When sketching or gluing shapes and colours on a piece of paper, for example, the designer encounters problems that need to be addressed. Decisions will have to be made. The designer will work with a lot of pictures showing references of garments, fabrics, a certain mood or atmosphere and characters, but without a form of processing them, those images are just a lot of information. The final costume drawing is the manifestation and artefact of this exploration process.

What matters is the process of thinking, making decisions and committing to ideas. Chapter 2 will introduce the reader to the tools available to the designer to explore ideas.

Collating Information

To ease into the exploration stage, it can be helpful and uplifting to collate all information, main reference and inspiration images, fabric swatches, and whatever else seems important, on to a pin wall, for example, if this has not been done already along the way. Alternatively, or even additionally, a moodboard could be created digitally with Photoshop, InDesign, Pinterest or Padlet, for example. The latter can be shared and collaborated on with other members of the creative team. Seeing everything at one glance can help the designer to make a start

This picture shows the process of designing costumes for an adaptation of *Alice in Wonderland* (1865, Lewis Carroll). On the pin-wall are key reference images for each character with a selection of fabric samples, giving ideas for colour and the quality of the desired materials.

at responding to the text. It might be a good idea, at this point, to reduce references down to those that really matter. This might be quite an intuitive process that is not necessarily logical or methodical. There might be something in the images that draws the designer's attention. It might be texture, the light, a very specific colour or shape. The designer needs to understand what it is that attracts their attention and be able to communicate this. These are vital considerations and the start of the decision-making process that brings the designer closer to developing a design concept.

Music and Conversations

Playing music associated with a production or research can help to create the right atmosphere to be creative. Conversations with the director or a peer might be helpful, if not even necessary. Conversations can be instrumental in unlocking creativity. Simply voicing concerns and uncertainties can help knowing how to address them or even realizing that they exist. It is often those concerns or insecurities that inhibit the creative flow.

USING WORD ASSOCIATIONS

It might be useful to go back to the text analysis toolbox introduced earlier in this chapter and explore those findings further, specifically the vocabularies and phrases. This could work well in combination with creating a mood-board or even a rough collage.

An example for a word association brainstorm could be created for *The Threepenny Opera* by Bertold Brecht in the following way:

The launchpad idea for this play could be power struggle or it could be moral chaos, for example, and the vocabularies noted down whilst reading the text could be religious, Victorian England, surreal, authoritarian, dark, shady, surreal, educational, corporate power, monumental and complex. These words give the designer a good starting point to look for shapes, textures, fabric and colours. Looking for pictures within fashion, architecture, interior design or art that represent the atmosphere of those words should be a good starting point.

Taking these words further, the designer might create a mood-board or collage.

A mood-board for a production of *The Threepenny Opera* (1928, Bertolt Brecht) by Bettina John. It is worth pointing out that this collage or mood-board does not solely consist of fashion and costume reference pictures, but architecture, textures, colour and architectural elements. When developing a costume concept, it is important to look beyond clothing to stimulate new approaches, innovation and to reduce replica.

Considering the 'World'

It is important to keep an awareness throughout the design process that a play is a fictional world; in other words, a concept or brief created by the creative team. Pretty much all the answers can be found in there. This world has its own logic to which the design and the directorial decisions have to adhere. If this is not the case, the production might run the risk of not being coherent or convincing to an audience. The key to a strong design and the success of a production is a fully formed world that has been sufficiently explored and then rigorously followed.

fabric manipulation,
texture inspired by wrought iron
referencing wallpaper of the time
light in appearance but weighs you down
delicate yet durable
weathered feel

TEXTURE

Viola Borsos developing ideas for *A Streetcar named Desire* (1951, Tennessee Williams), as part of the UAL Costume Design for Performance course, 2020.

A decision on the kind of world will have to be made in the beginning of the design process. It is important to keep the script and its essence in mind and to avoid imposing ideas and aesthetics on to it. A script can serve as a platform for a creative team, but the creative team needs to be mindful when negotiating the limits to the interpretation of this script. In general terms, a world could be surreal, abstract, symbolic, fantastic, realistic or a combination of those but within that, there is a lot of detail to navigate. Once the world is clear, all questions regarding the design need to be tested against the rules of this world. Having said that, at this stage, the designer might not be entirely clear about this world yet. This is partly what the next stage is about: the exploration stage, which includes the exploration of the world, its understanding in practical terms, in colours, shapes and, later on, in actual clothing. A creative team can put a lot of thought into a production and be very thorough in creating the world and yet not know if this world will be convincing or even interesting, especially if it is unusual or complex, or untried. This moment requires trust. An open-minded approach to experimentation will certainly make this process better and more enjoyable.

Knowing the Non-Negotiables

It might well be the case that a lot of major design decisions have been made in the beginning of a project or before the costume designer has become involved – maybe in a preliminary conversation with the director and set designer or there is a brief outlining the main parameters. The section 'Parameters and How to Navigate Them' in Chapter 3 will go into more detail on how a design concept has been shaped before the designer has even started working on it. The brief might clearly state that the costumes need to follow the fashion of a specific period, or this particular point might be negotiable and could, therefore, be substantially shaped by the designer. In this case, the designer could

have a lot of fun coming up with fantastic ideas. However, the designer would not want to forget that the costumes need to fulfil aspects of functionality. Furthermore, the designer has a lot of responsibility, not only with regard to the costumes looking good and suiting the actor, but the design also needs to work within the overall production concept. After concluding the research, the designer should commence the interpretation of any given parameters and the research findings in their own unique way.

Storyboarding

Every act or scene could have a slightly different atmosphere and angle on the overall design concept. Costumes in one act could be much darker, while another act could be quite surreal, with regard to both the design and staging of the play. At some point, the designer might need to involve the director, set designer and maybe even the lighting and sound designer in this conversation. A more in-depth introduction to storyboarding can be found in Chapter 4.

Developing an Overall Design Concept

After the initial research period has been concluded, in most cases, the development of an overall design concept will follow. The designer will settle on colours, shapes and the general mood for the different scenes and acts, specifically if they differ. The next step after that is the development of the designs for the individual characters and how their costume will work within the overall concept. This will be explored in more detail in Chapter 4. It is good to keep in mind that more research will be necessary at various stages throughout the design process. This might be more in-depth or very specific research and can sometimes involve the designer visiting relevant places or specialist libraries or research centres.

Brenda Mejia utilizing collaging as a tool for developing a design concept for *A Streetcar named Desire* (1951, Tennessee Williams), as part of the UAL Costume Design for Performance course, 2020.

A BIT OF PRACTICAL ADVICE

On Inspiration

Inspiration is certainly key to the design process. It promotes motivation and gets the designer excited. A lack of inspiration can be frustrating and a real hindrance, which is why the designer has to ensure a process that allows for inspiration to appear. For example, playing with images, colours, shapes and silhouettes or reading about characters, the playwright, places or historical events can have an inspirational effect. The brain seems to be most creative when relaxed, when occupied with a task similar to playing and when a state of flow has been reached. The subconscious then starts developing ideas in the background. That can be a reason why people find the creative process so magical. However, the design process involves hours of work and dedication. A method to follow gives a sense of familiarity in an otherwise quite tumultuous and uncertain life that a costume designer tends to live. While some people thrive on uncertainty and the ever-closer approaching deadline, others actually really enjoy planning ahead. Both ways will have a method to them, if they lead to good results. It is important to find out what works best and is sustainable. Some designers enjoy reading a script over and over again, while others enjoy looking through magazines, cutting out images and working them into collages.

On Routine

It is worth stressing the importance of having a good routine: it helps in getting through times when life is more challenging and distraction is great. Having a good breakfast, doing some light exercise, maybe a morning run or walk before starting to work, for example. Taking breaks, having a coffee or tea, taking lunch, doing some stretching or even a brief conversation with a friend or colleague can help tremendously and can become a vital part of a successful routine. For most people, certainly creative people, the place they work in is very important and, sometimes more importantly, how it is organized. Some people might like it very organized and tidy up their workstation every time they start working. Other people might need a little bit of life around them to feel motivated. While chaos might help a few, generally, having a friendly and organized environment tends to help enormously. A very messy place, however, can become quite the distraction.

Sometimes a change of scene might be helpful. In that case a local cafe or library might make a difference; a place further away that involves a walk or travel, a friend's house, a co-working space or the park, for example. In fact, a walk can do wonders after a prolonged period of concentration, a long meeting or simply a lack of motivation. Being a costume designer can be a challenge socially. It is a constant change between being with a lot of people in sometimes stressful and high-pressure environments and long stretches of working alone, only occasionally seeing the rest of the creative team. That would be why designers often share studios with other designers or creatives.

Part of a good routine is staying informed, reading relevant texts on a regular basis, following other artists, finding mentors, building relationships, possibly watching relevant films and television and, of course, going to the theatre. All of these activities need to somehow fit into the busy schedule of a costume designer. Granted, this is not always easy or possible; however, understanding the importance of stimulation is crucial to remaining inspired.

THE INSPIRATION LIBRARY

It is highly recommended to pursue interests and collect images and materials unrelated to current projects. Images and materials can be organized and archived into an inspiration library and consulted if and when needed – it can be digital, as well as collections of books, materials and objects. Holding an object, such as a stone, a piece of wood, a sculpture or a shell, can be transformational and hugely inspiring. Inspiration works through all senses.

ORGANIZING INFORMATION

When talking about an effective routine, organization has to be part of the conversation. Although creative people are often portrayed as less organized, they are not more or less organized than anybody else. Everybody, however, will have to develop their own systems. Storing digitally seems to become more relevant and it is, therefore, worth saying a few words about that. First and foremost, not all data need to be stored in the so-called Cloud. In fact, it might be wise to additionally store your information on an external hard-drive, which is always accessible and only by the person to whom it belongs. It is private, tends to be very stable and is, potentially, a more reliable storage form than the computer itself. But, more importantly, every document should have a back-up and should be organized in a logical manner, just like the designer's tools, materials and drawings should be.

Studio of freelance costume designer and maker Elizabeth Real (Twisted Reality Studio). Every designer will get to the point of accepting that a certain organization is necessary. It saves time, space and allows the designer to focus on the design rather than being distracted by a disorganized studio. This organization does not necessarily have to appear tidy to every other person, but it needs to have some logic to it that eases the designer's workflow.

EXERCISES

This book offers a selection of exercises that the reader can take as a starting point to explore the design process and develop their own approach to it. They can be built and expanded on, if desired. They can be done individually or, in the case of the reader wanting to explore the design process as a whole and in more depth, a script could be chosen and the design process, detailed in this book, could be followed as suggested. In this case, the exercises and tools proposed can all be applied to the same script and speculative design project and followed in sequence.

Exercise 1: Help to Stay Focused When Conducting Research

Conducting research can feel overwhelming. Setting yourself a task and restricting what to look for can help staying focused. The following suggestions aim to give you an idea that you are invited to expand upon and depart from.

Use a play of your choice and gather the following images relevant to it:

- At least two to three images that are not of a piece of clothing or a costume; for example, a photo of a building or a painting of nature or a piece of furniture.
- Two to three images that are surfaces or textures. They do not have to be fabric; in fact, a variety of other materials with textures would be favourable.

Exercise 2: Help to Stay Focused When Conducting Research

Depending on the play, you can create a specific list of references to look for and restrict the time you will spend looking for them. It could be anything that feels useful. The following list is an example for a period play. Please create a useful list yourself and, if applicable, base it on the play you chose for the speculative design project.

- Three to five images of servants, if useful with different responsibilities.
- Three images of a lady of aristocratic background.
- Three images of a working-class woman, if useful with different responsibilities.
- Three images of a working-class man, if useful with different responsibilities.
- Three different male and female hairstyles.
- Images of how to tie a men's tie/cravat.

Exercise 3: Finding Inspiration and Developing and Furthering Interests

Places
Go to a local library, bookstore, second-hand bookstore or flea market and start looking at books and objects that spark your interest. Pick a random book or object and begin your journey. Find out more about the author or creator.

Other Artists
Find a couple of artists or designers you have never heard of, and spend some time studying their work. Why do you like them? Make sense of why you are attracted by certain aesthetics, forms, shapes and colours. Make notes.

Zooming-In
If possible, visit a museum or gallery that showcases fashion or costume and pick one item that you are particularly attracted to. This could also be an online exhibition, a virtual tour through a museum or, in fact, a picture of a dress, if none of the above is available. Investigate why you are attracted to it. Write down your thoughts and insights.

Observation

Over the course of a week, pay attention to the use of colour, a material or a particular fabric that you encounter in your day-to-day life. Jot down your observations in a notebook. Observe how it reacts to light, observe the drape of the fabric, the shape of an object. What caught your attention? How does it make you feel?

You can start a book of ideas and gather information of this nature in it.

Exercise 4: Scene Breakdown

Take a script of your choice and divide it into acts, scenes and units, and make notes of as much information as you deem relevant, using the scene breakdown chart. It is recommendable to take the same script as a basis for the following exercises, as this will help you to understand how these tools function in combination. Once you have completed this, it is worth trying these exercises, using a variety of other scripts, such as a modern play or an opera libretto.

Exercise 5: Mapping the Appearance of Characters Throughout a Play

Using the same script, go through it again, scene by scene, and track the appearances of characters in a chart, as suggested earlier in this chapter.

Exercise 6: Character's Quotations' Chart

Using the same script, identify comments of characters that concern other characters. Use the chart introduced earlier to organize your findings.

Exercise 7: Understanding Themes and Motifs Through Vocabulary

Using the same script, extract words from it that speak to you and note them down on a piece of paper. Start playing with them by combining and adding new ones. Find associations. It should feel like a brainstorm and produce a sort of mind-map that can be referred to throughout the design process, especially when at a loss for ideas, inspiration or indeed direction.

Exercise 8: Launchpad Ideas

After having completed exercises 4–7, it should now be possible to identify some of the themes in a script that interest you. You can now find pertinent words or phrases that you could use as a starting point to develop design ideas from. Look for words that spark your imagination, combine several words into exciting visual cues, create word plays, contradiction, exaggeration or tension. Think of texture, colour, shape and silhouette.

Jean.

- Clothes not as l
  countess.
- Has overcoat –
- 'sensitive'.
- Cigar
- smirky /contro
- Wants to ache
- big dreams

- rela
- unbu

2
PRACTICAL TECHNIQUES FOR EXPLORING DESIGN

THE MAGIC OF EXPLORING

Looking at pictures and thinking or talking about design concepts will reach its limits. Equally, starting to narrow down costume ideas while they are still forming can feel forced. Characters will not have been developed at this stage and still need careful consideration. The solution is the insertion of an additional step. Before a concept can be developed, ideas and characters need to be explored and tested. This chapter will introduce a range of effective tools that most designers use in some way or another in order to explore their ideas. However, different designers develop different approaches and pretty much every production means starting over again, challenging and unlearning what worked before. Developing good routines and useful methods, such as those proposed in this chapter, make it a lot more likely to consistently achieve great results.

Sitting in front of a blank piece of paper, waiting for answers to come, will probably be the least successful way to explore ideas. Exploring is less about conceptualizing and more about testing ideas in a safe environment. The only aim of this process should be to come to conclusions and make discoveries and decisions, and not to create beautiful works of art ready to be exhibited. It will take the pressure off to keep that in mind.

OPPOSITE: Megan Stilwell exploring design ideas for *Miss Julie* (1889, August Strindberg), as part of the UAL Costume Design for Performance short course, 2018.

This process should be playful and enjoyable, allowing creative channels to open up. Therefore, it will be a good start to use imagery, materials and resources found through preceding research or in the personal inspiration library that was introduced in Chapter 1. Some designers might explore shapes and colour in the form of collages, cutting out details and textures from magazines and gluing them on paper. Others might play with images on the computer, doing essentially the same thing. In both cases, the advantage is that they directly utilize the images found when researching, rather than starting with a blank page, which might confront some designers with sudden insecurities.

Some designers have built a collection of costumes or have access to a costumes store or hire. This allows for testing ideas on a mannequin or even on a model. Taking pictures of the results and drawing over them might be a successful method. Others might use the photographs as a study to help with sketching and drawing later on; this could be particularly useful for complex drapes or costumes that break away from the norm. Whichever method used, all of them engage the brain in a process of thinking and ideas can be generated and explored further, decisions made and solutions found. Throughout this process, anticipation and confidence to draw might have built up and will then be a moment of joy rather than frustration.

It will not be sufficient to only present research images as a design concept to the creative team, makers and actors. First, this is not an effective way of communicating a design, as it leaves too much room for interpretation and, second, it is rather unlikely that it will result in an original and coherent design concept. There is a need to respond to images in a creative way, processing and developing them into a design concept, otherwise it might just be a good piece of research. Furthermore, there is a need to extract relevant information and, eventually, put it into a form that communicates the design effectively to the director

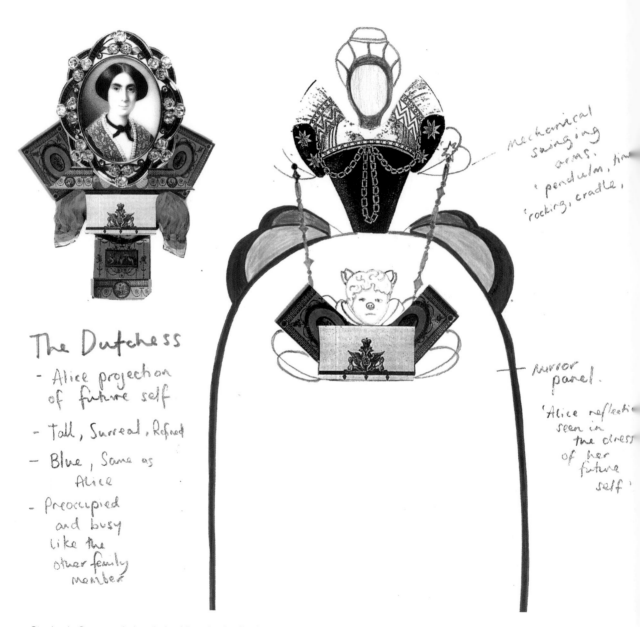

mechanical swinging arms.
· pendulum, tim
· rocking, cradle,

The Duchess

- Alice projection of future self

- Tall, Surreal, Refined

- Blue, Same as Alice

- Preoccupied and busy like the other family members

mirror panel.

'Alice reflecti seen in the dress of her future self'

Stephanie Overs exploring design ideas for the Duchess of *Alice in Wonderland* (1865, Lewis Carroll), as part of the UAL Costume Design for Performance short course, 2019.

and, later on, to the makers and actors. Reference images alone will not suffice here. A design presentation can take many forms and might not be a traditional costume drawing, but instead consists of pictures of drapes on mannequins and some notes accompanying these photographs. How to compile and communicate a design effectively will be expanded on in Chapter 3.

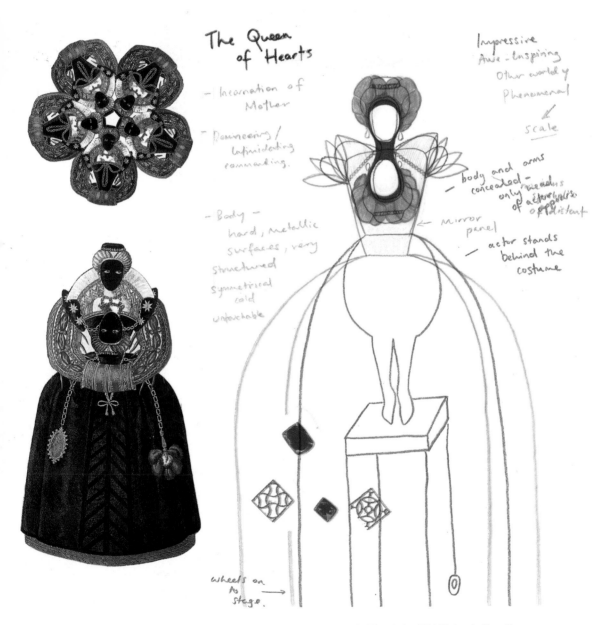

Stephanie Overs exploring design ideas for the Queen of Hearts of *Alice in Wonderland* (1865, Lewis Carroll).

The Different Tools

Designer and maker Paulina Knol exploring design ideas for Count Almaviva, a character from Rossini's classic opera *The Barber of Seville* (1816), as part of the UAL Costume Design for Performance short course, 2019.

COLLAGE-MAKING

Collages can be made in infinitely different ways, which depends not least on what is being explored. The examples of collages accompanying this section show a range of approaches. Some of them focus on the overall design concept, mood and atmosphere. Several focus on design elements, such as texture, silhouette, shape, pattern and colour. Others focus on character qualities, such as body shape and posture, the character's attitude and even facial expressions. The latter explore the character itself and constitute a form of character development.

Collages could be made on paper, using magazines, fabric, materials and coloured paper, or digitally with the help of software such as Photoshop or equivalents such as Affinity. Some designers have mastered using various apps specifically made for the iPad or other tablets. A lot of designers enjoy using tablets, which have paved the way for new possibilities. A combination of these methods and tools might be a good solution.

Making collages could have several functions. In some cases they can be a tool to explore specific questions such as whether a jacket would work with a pair of denims or with suit trousers, or indeed a

Design process by set and costume designer Bettina John for the dance piece *Everything and Nothing* by choreographer James Cousins (2012). These examples explore textures and shapes for dance by means of collages, using architecture magazine cut-outs.

Design process by set and costume designer Bettina John for the dance piece *Rites of Spring* (2016, choreographer Ben Duke of Lost Dog). These examples explore design for dance by means of collages, using small pieces of fabric and arranging them on the page, in a way suggesting the human body. The patterns on the fabric samples used here would ordinarily be relatively small in proportion to the human body but appear now much bigger, an effect that might be an interesting starting point for a design.

skirt. The computer can be a very practical tool here and might be favoured in this case. Creating collages using magazine cut-outs, on the other hand, might be a more freeing exercise, possibly less focused and more playful and intuitive. This could be an earlier exercise; for example, to break up the research process and generate ideas. Furthermore ideas could be generated by using fabric or other materials in a collage, which will change the material's impact, due to the different proportion; or, architecture magazine cut-outs can suggest textures, a type of fabric, new ways of using it or unusual

materials. This method can be an ideas generator or lead to unusual design choices, far removed from the conventional use of clothing and patterns. The approach to collage-making, techniques applied and materials used will affect its outcome.

Furthermore, different design briefs require different approaches. Designing for an abstract dance piece, for example, allows or even demands a freer, more generous design approach; making a collage using bold blocks of colour cut-outs from magazines might be the right direction here. A period costume design brief, on the other hand, requires more in-depth historical costume research and accuracy. In this case, tracing reference images and manipulating those might be more helpful. Collage-making is not only a tool to explore ideas but also to understand and explore the design elements, which is fundamental to the designer. The designer needs to have a good understanding of what the various methods and tools can achieve, what they offer to the process and when they can be limiting.

Bettina John exploring designs for Rossini's *The Barber of Seville* (1816). This series of digital collages and watercolour drawings gives an insight into the design process from exploring ideas to the final costume drawing of the character Figaro, which is a watercolour drawing on paper in this example. With the rise of digital drawing, it is more common now to work both digitally and on paper, and combine the two.

Eva Buryakovsky exploring design ideas for Gwendolen (left) and Lady Bracknell (right) of Oscar Wilde's *The Importance of Being Earnest* (1895), as part of the UAL Costume Design for Performance short course, 2020.

GARMENT AND FABRIC DRAPING ON A MANNEQUIN

Draping on the mannequin, often simply referred to as the stand, or draping on the human body itself, with materials, fabric or clothes, can be both a means to test ideas and to generate them. Draping can be very useful to explore shapes, silhouettes, colours and patterns. It is unbeatable when wanting to test the drape of a particular fabric or a combination of a blouse and a pair of trousers or a jacket over a dress. Regarding these questions, draping can be much more effective than trying to answer them in a two-dimensional drawing. Drawings and, even more so, collages will always leave space for the imagination, which make these methods so appealing. However, some situations require the designer to test ideas three-dimensionally and with the actual materials. When dressing a mannequin with a blouse and a skirt, for example, the effect is instantly visible. It is possible to see the effect of a silhouette, a fabric or, more specifically, a pattern from up close and from further away, which is important to find out. The effect of a pattern, for example, could get completely lost when looking at it from further away. For that reason, it is important to keep the average distance between stage and audience in mind. This is particularly relevant in the case of larger theatre settings for which some details or prints may need to be exaggerated to be seen. Equally, something that looks like a pattern up-close could appear more like a texture from a distance, which might or might not be a desired effect.

Draping allows for a much more three-dimensional, possibly even sculptural, approach to costume. When conducted skilfully, it can help to develop conventional garments into something quite unusual. Draping is very common amongst fashion designers, as it is a great tool to work through much more abstract ideas. It is particularly helpful when trying to develop experimental designs. Costume designers might use it to develop designs for modern dance or opera. In fact, this design process bears close resemblance to the process of designing a capsule fashion collection. Draping is also a great tool to develop the actual designs, especially when an interest in the recycling and re-using of garments and fabrics exists. In this case, garments could be explored on the stand, with regard to their potential to appear differently from how they were meant to appear.

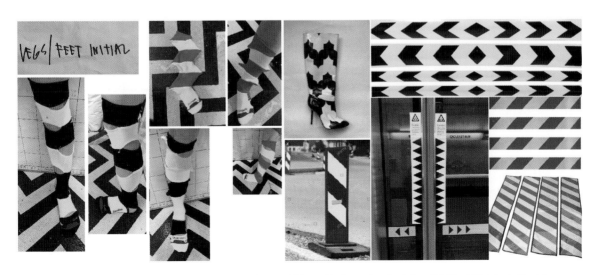

Design process by multi-disciplinary designer Louise Gray for Wayne McGregor's adaptation (2019) of Christoph Gluck's *Orpheus and Eurydice* (1762).

These images show how multi-disciplinary designer Louise Gray utilized the draping tool in her design process for Wayne McGregor's adaptation (2019) of Christoph Gluck's *Orpheus and Eurydice* (1762). As demonstrated here, draping fabrics can also be done on a live model rather than a mannequin, which allows for a lot more possibilities, such as using the legs, arms and the head (model Aminat D. Seriki).

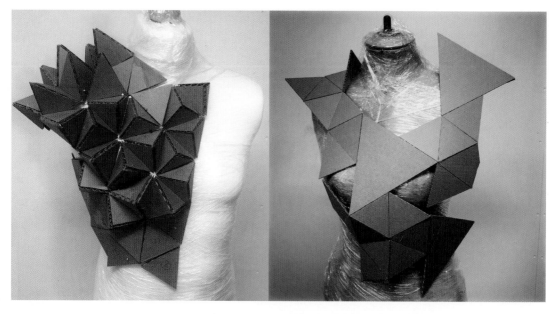

Examples of the design process of wearable sculpture artist Daphne Karstens. It is possible to use other materials apart from fabric and to achieve compelling designs. Some materials might be the starting point for a design exploration.

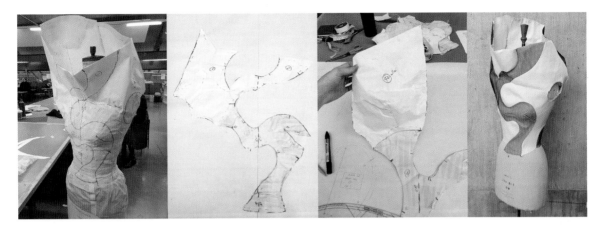

It is possible to use paper to drape on the mannequin, as this example of the design process of costume designer and maker Sophie Ruth Donaldson demonstrates.

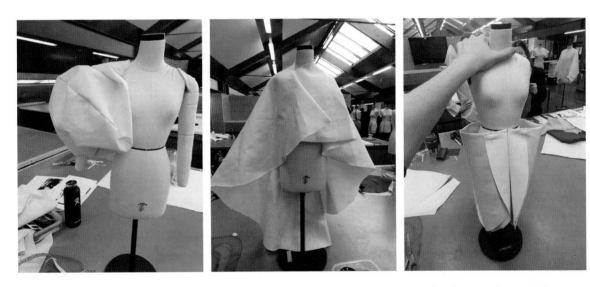

These examples show draping on a small stand, no more than 30cm in height. Sophie Ruth Donaldson made use of this method to save time and material trialling some design ideas in 3D.

WRITING

Writing and the playing with words can be another great tool to generate and develop design ideas. Chapter 1 has already introduced the reader to this concept. Writing can be utilized in this way throughout the design process but can adopt various other forms. Apart from brainstorming and mindmapping, it can also simply be used by the designer to organize their thoughts. At various times throughout the design process, this will be an incredibly useful exercise and help to streamline it. Rather than thinking about ideas, noting them down forces the designer to clarify them. This is the first step to testing them. Furthermore, regularly writing about design processes, formulating thoughts into texts or critically investigating a subject matter through writing, will improve analytical and methodical thinking. Reflecting on their work makes the designer less likely to be one-time lucky and instead create, consistently, high-quality work. Sufficient and clear notes can also help the designer to learn from mistakes when looking back at past projects.

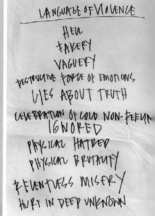

These images show documents of the design process of multi-disciplinary designer Louise Gray for Wayne McGregor's adaptation (2019) of Christoph Gluck's *Orpheus and Eurydice* (1762) for the English National Opera, London. Gray frequently uses the writing tool and its visual potential to explore and support her ideas and designs.

DRAWING

Drawing, or rather sketching, is a common tool used by designers to visualize and memorize ideas. Some designers, comfortable in the medium of drawing, however, use it as a form of exploring. When exploring through drawing, the focus lies on the thinking while doing, similar to doodling or brainstorming. Those preliminary drawings could even be rough sketches and unfinished scribbles, more often than not, ready to be dismissed. It is important to distinguish sketching from drawing at this point. Sketching signifies an explorative element, whereas, in this context, drawing is the visualization of a well-formed idea – the costume drawing. However, a costume drawing is also just a means to an end and not the end product itself. The end product is the costume on stage, worn by the performer and lit in the right way.

When attempting to produce the final costume drawing, the designer might realize that several more attempts need to follow and the process of exploring continues. It is important not to get frustrated at this point but to understand that this is still a form of exploration that aims toward organizing all the various thoughts and ideas. Before the designer makes the final costume drawing, there will often have been a long period of trial and error. The final drawing will rarely be the first one. Experienced designers will know that and will have gone through this process many times before and, hence, will not get too concerned about it. To some extent, they have become used to it.

The final costume drawing marks the end point of the design exploration. For some designers, the transition from exploration to the final drawing might happen organically; other designers quite consciously end the exploration process and commence with their final costume drawings. Furthermore, some designers keep exploring throughout the costume realization process and other designers stop exploring when starting their final drawings, which will then barely change throughout the realization process. Whether comfortable with drawing or not, it is a useful tool that can be learnt and practised. The next section takes the reader through the basics of drawing, not least to make this point.

A page of Sophie Ruth Donaldson's sketchbook, showing design idea sketches for dance costumes.

A page of Sophie Ruth Donaldson's sketchbook, showing design idea sketches for costumes for the dance performance *Stunners* (2019, Tamar & Jo).

DRAWING: THE BASICS

Moving into the drawing stage can be challenging. While the mood-board keeps options open, drawing forces the designer into making decisions. This might contribute to initial concerns when starting to draw out ideas and not, as often concluded, the lack of drawing skills. Drawing, like any other skill, can be learnt and practised, if enough time and energy is dedicated to it. Studying and practising it will enable any aspiring designer to draw a costume. However, a beautiful drawing is not always a good costume design. What counts is the information the drawing contains. A drawing could be beautiful but not fit the brief or contain enough information for the creative team to understand the costume designer's vision or makers to commence the realization process. It might not fit in with the rest of the costume designs, characters or scenes. A good costume drawing needs to communicate vital information effectively. As long as it does that, it is less important how beautiful or charming the drawing is. The following section focuses, therefore, on those aspects of drawing relevant to achieving a successful costume drawing.

Costume design for Cecily of *The Importance of Being Earnest* (1895, Oscar Wilde) with references for textures, colour and mood by costume designer Delilah Bannister. A costume design mostly consists of more than the costume drawing. It should also give ideas for the materials and can contain reference images.

Considering the Body

Fundamental to costume drawing is the understanding of the body underneath. The designer needs to consider the qualities of the body, such as its posture, body type and shape, age and attitude, before they can draw the costume on to it. While over the course of a designer's professional life a certain drawing style is being developed, and the focus might move away from anatomical correctness, certainly when beginning to draw, looking at the body itself is a vital exercise. Resorting to specialist books to study the body in more detail will be very useful and attending life-drawing classes, when starting out as a designer, is highly recommended. The following section will go into more detail regarding the qualities of the body and how making decisions on them will impact upon the development of the characters.

Costume designs for *Madam Butterfly* (1904, Giacomo Puccini, libretto Giuseppe Giacosa and Luigi Illica) by set and costume designer Nicky Shaw.

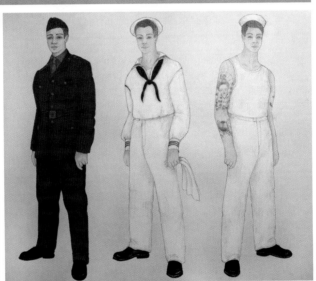

BODY TYPES AND SHAPES

The designer might begin their character development by choosing an appropriate body type and shape. What makes people into unique individuals is the unique body they were born with and their unique story, lifestyle and habits that have manifested in their body. The designer needs to come to an understanding of the character's life and journey, their psychology, emotions, background, upbringing and lifestyle. Some of this information will be found in the script, some will be discussed with the director and some, possibly many, discoveries and decisions the designer will have to make for themselves. At this stage, it might be helpful to look back at the various images of people found during the research phase and investigate them in terms of these questions. A few of the depictions of people might speak to how the designer imagines a character. On the other hand, they might give the designer a starting point on how

Orpheus

Corset
Leather and
Chiffon

Venus
Sky Ingram

Sandals

Train

Orpheus

Breast-Plate
and Back
made of
Leather
with
Leather straps
at shoulder
and Leather
Skirt

Cupi
Keri Fug

Feather Wi

Trouser
cut with low
crotch -
wide at
thighs, over. l

Wedge Ankl.
Boots with
Rosettes

a character could be developed. It is a two-way process: finding the right pictures and being led by those found. Additionally, the designer should revisit the scene breakdown chart and the character quotations to gather all necessary information and facts on the characters.

There is a potential slight difference between the body type and the actual shape of the body. The body type is what a person has been born with or is genetically more prone to, being tall or small, for example. The costume designer can go ahead and imagine a character of a certain body type, but there is nothing that can be done if the eventual choice of actor differs from that. The body shape, on the other hand, is subject to lifestyle choices and habits, such as diet, activities,

profession or attitude, as well as much less controllable factors, such as emotions and mental health. These are the qualities that the costume designer and actor could manipulate. While there are limitations to that, there are still very good reasons for the designer to have thoughts on those qualities. Granted, the best-case scenario is when the designer has knowledge of the cast when designing the costume. This would allow them to take the actor's body shape and type into account. But beside this option, the designer might influence the director's cast choice with their costume drawing. Additionally, the costume drawing might impact upon how the actor interprets a character. In many cases, the designer should be in the position to pre-empt the cast choice,

Costume drawings by set and costume designer Nicky Shaw for *Orpheus* (1647, composer Luigi Rossi, directed by Keith Warner). The designer applied various different stances and attitudes here to suit the individual characters.

by doing thorough research and having in-depth conversations with the director. Either way, the designer should feel confident that there are many qualities that can be manipulated very effectively by using the costume. Together with the abilities of the actor to control their body, it can have a tremendously transformative effect.

ATTITUDE, POSTURE AND STANCE

Body type and shape are closely intertwined with the posture and attitude of a character and have to be considered at the same time. Reading a person's appearance can be understood as layers of information: the body type and shape being the first, on top of which is their posture, on top of this their attitude and the last layer is their clothing.

Adding up this information will allow for a remarkable insight into a person and their life.

Posture can be understood in two different ways: there is the posture that a person has adopted permanently and then there is the posture or stance a person has in a moment. They might not differ much or not at all, or they might have to be differentiated for a good reason. For example, a character might normally be very confident but is being put in a difficult situation in the story and responds with insecurity. That might mean that their ordinary posture is one of openness and confidence, hence upright and strong, but a situation in a particular scene might have compromised their appearance somewhat. It might manifest only in their facial expression or in

card no 6   The Queen   The White Rabbit   The Duchess   Alice   The Mad Hatter   The Mouse   The cheshire cat

Costume designs by set and costume designer Bettina John for an adaptation of *Alice in Wonderland* (1865, Lewis Carroll). The designer applied various different body shapes, stances and attitudes here to emphasize the individual characters.

a gesture. A posture that a person has adopted permanently tells the onlooker how somebody feels generally about themselves and how they relate to their environment. A character could be permanently sad, which could have manifested in hanging shoulders, for example. This might not be easily reversed, whereas a situation that made somebody sad momentarily might manifest in their body in a slightly different and, most importantly, not a permanent way.

Posture also allows for judgement on somebody's age. An older person might not stand as upright compared to a young person and their body might not appear as strong any more, unless they are a particularly fit older person. The degree of fitness and type of daily activity will, most likely, be reflected in the body. Somebody who works as a farmer, for example might appear stronger than somebody working indoors, seated in front of a computer every day. However, there could be a scenario where a character does exactly this kind of sedentary work but also goes to the fitness studio every day, resulting in a fitter body. Character development would need to take these considerations into account.

It is important to be aware of the character's context, their cultural background and the time in which the play is set, as these factors will have an impact on how qualities such as body shape and attitude will be read. Furthermore, it is important

to be careful when resorting to stereotypes and to be aware of what is currently acceptable and what could be perceived as offensive.

Last, but not least, it is worth mentioning that, with regard to costume drawing, some postures work better than others, for practical reasons; for example, to show the costume in the best way. A lot of designers adopt a range of postures and stick to them, after having learnt to draw them effortlessly. Many designers make these choices intuitively but will have initially spent more time making conscious decisions, which is important.

Age

A character's posture and stance are the main adjustments the designer can make when drawing a character of old age, but there are a few more. Proportions of the body, skin and the face change with age too. Muscles might look more defined when getting older, but then tend to shrink with age, exposing more of the bone structure underneath. Skin might appear thinner and will, of course, show more signs of ageing, such as wrinkles. A person's body, especially when more mature, shows how they lived their life, their life experience, perhaps, wisdom and generosity, a life full of joy and happiness, or perhaps, one of unhappiness and greed. There is great potential to develop the character by considering these qualities carefully; however, these qualities cannot be utilized in the costume itself. They are a tool to develop characters and to communicate them in the drawing to the director and actor, which is, in fact, if successful, a tremendous achievement. In that way, the costume designer does not only develop a costume but also actively participates

Costume drawings for an adaptation of *Alice in Wonderland* (1865, Lewis Carroll) by set and costume designer Bettina John. It is important to consider the age of a character when designing and eventually drawing the final design.

Costume drawings for *Hansel and Gretel* (1812, Brothers Grimm) by set and costume designer Jason Southgate. The designer achieved great character representation in these illustrations by considering age and body shape, attitude and facial expressions.

in the shaping of a character. Then, there is, of course, the costume itself. Most people change their way of dressing over time and adjust it to their age and situation. Having developed a good understanding of a character, including their age, attitude and body shape, will help finding solutions for their costume, as this process helps the designer to picture the character and bring them to life.

GESTURES AND FACIAL EXPRESSION

As gestures and facial expressions are usually momentary, they might not necessarily say much about a character fundamentally but more about the situation a character is in. However, it could still be a tool for a designer to explore character and communicate this to the creative team and cast. Giving a character a friendly and open face, for example, could indicate the character's positive nature and help to communicate the designer's suggestions about a character to the director and actor. In any case, the designer will have to make a choice on the facial expression and gesture, no matter how small or big they are, and this choice needs to add up to the whole picture. Gestures might be of particular interest to the designer beyond the development of the character. The designer might make a generic choice about a gesture for practical reasons with regard to the drawing itself. A certain gesture might allow for sleeves to be seen in a better way, for example. Equally, the designer might apply a neutral facial expression to keep it simple. Most experienced designers might not think about facial expressions and gestures much and, in reality, there will not always be enough time for it; however, it is worth spending some time learning to control these qualities.

No Man's Land

Hirst - Act One

No Man's Land

Spooner

Costume designs for *No Man's Land* (1974, Harold Pinter) by theatre designer Bek Palmer.

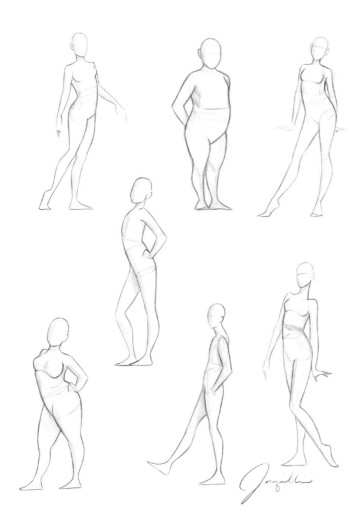

Figurines by designer
and illustrator Jocquillin
Shaunté Nayoan.

of developing the character. If the costume drawing effectively communicates information about the character and costume, nobody will care how it was created.

The choice of figurine is essentially making decisions on the qualities of the body, laid out above, and should, therefore, be done with great care. Whether the right or wrong figurine is used will have an impact on the design. This applies not only when choosing the right body type and shape, posture and attitude, but also when considering the style of the figurine. Using a fashion figurine, as opposed to a more realistic body shape, will most likely be less useful. In most cases, the fashion figurine has been a rather unrealistic portrayal of the human body, created in a way to make a dress look perfect. It is often a stylization of the human body, reducing character purposefully to allow the fashion design to stand out. This is the opposite of what a costume design and character drawing aim to achieve. The designer needs to consider the degree of stylization a figurine underwent and what this stands for. The style of the figurine will support

The Figurine and on Using Templates

Considering the character, as laid out above, while capturing these thoughts in a drawing, can be overwhelming. It is not unusual to be unsure about how to get started and to delay it by searching for better references. When this happens, it is best to make it easier by using figurine templates. While some people might deem this cheating, others using a template are already thinking about the character, rather than getting frustrated with the task of getting body proportions right. A costume drawing is, first and foremost, a means to an end, a tool, and not a demonstration of how well the designer can draw. In fact, the process of choosing a figurine could already be the start

a more realistic or much more stylized approach to the body; either of these options can be effectively utilized by the designer.

Using a figurine particular to a period could also be helpful. The twenties, forties, fifties or eighties, for example, had very particular figurines, as each period had its own body ideals. The twenties, for example, favoured an androgynous body, whereas the eighties preferred a healthy and fitter body shape. Using those figurines as a basis for the design can be a tool to bring out a specific period. Furthermore, there is a lot to learn from studying figurines and fashion plates of the various periods, as they often have a high degree of stylization and depict the ideal version of the body and fashion of the time. This can be very helpful in understanding the essential idealistic aesthetic of a period.

There is a great choice of figurine templates available online, but it might be a good idea for the student, and also the designer, to develop a set of figurines for themselves. It is a good exercise, as well as a way to make character drawings look more unique. Furthermore, having a good range of figurine templates will come in very handy when the schedule gets busier. A simple and quick way to create one could be by tracing over photographs of people, fashion plates and illustrations. However, when using photographs, it might be more appropriate, in some instances, to develop it further into a less naturalistic version. Additionally, it is most likely that the person was photographed at an angle to the camera, which results in a slight distortion of the body, particularly visible when traced. In the case of the upper body being closer to the camera, for example, the legs may appear foreshortened and, therefore, disrupt the body's proportions and take away from the drawing itself. Despite these challenges, it can be very useful, and it is indeed common practice, to use photographs of the actual cast as a template for a costume drawing, if those are available. These could be printed out and used as a base to work costume ideas on top or they could be manipulated in photo-editing programs such as Photoshop. It could be incredibly useful, before expanding into a more individual drawing, to experiment with the actor's natural shape by adding padding or a corset, for example, which shape the body in different ways, or add wigs, facial hair, make-up or prosthetics.

Costume drawings for *Hairspray* (2002, Marc Shaiman, Mark O'Donnell) set in 1960s Baltimore by theatre designer Bek Palmer.

Brenda Mejia exploring design ideas for Oscar Wilde's *The Importance of Being Earnest* (1985), as part of the UAL Costume Design for Performance short course, 2020.

Developing and Using Different Drawing Styles

While designers will inevitably develop their unique drawing style over time, this might still differ from production to production. The designer might need to consider the style in which a character and their costume is drawn in order to match the style of the production, not least because the style of a costume drawing determines, to a surprisingly high degree, the design itself. A naturalistic play from the 1890s, for example, with the brief to design in period costume, might ask for a more realistic drawing style, whereas a modern opera for a stylized one. That could be expressed through exaggerated body parts and silhouettes, particular application of paint or even simply the quality of line. The style will emerge in the process, in conversations, pictures and research. This emergence might not always be noticeable and, like so many aspects of designing, not necessarily be in the consciousness of the designer.

Looking at the iconic costume drawings from 1920s Bauhaus artists, for example, shows an emphasis on geometric shapes. They are bold and far removed from the realistic body. The characters in those drawings are stylized, maybe to emphasize only certain aspects of a person, maybe to stereotype or maybe simply to experiment with shape, form, dynamics, light or colour. Using drawing in this way allows for more experimentation in the design process. It also indicates a more experimental form of theatre. When imagining a production with abstract costumes, more stylized images, language and movements will automatically come to mind, rather than naturalistic dialogue, for example. Character development seems possible only to a certain degree and, in fact, might not be desirable. Watching recordings of Bauhaus

productions will show that they are, indeed, with little to no text, that they are music-centric and accompanied with a much more abstract body language. This approach to costume drawing seems beneficial for visually driven productions, maybe productions that have music or dance at their core, such as contemporary dance or modern opera. It could also be a useful style for surreal theatre or mime.

Having mentioned experimental theatre and form, it might be worth touching briefly on this vast field of study: form, style and genre. A production is not only of a specific genre but also in a particular

Costume design for *The Rites of Spring* (2016, Ben Duke of Lost Dog) by set and costume designer Bettina John. The designer focused here on the overall ensemble look, shapes, silhouettes and colour. Character becomes a more abstract idea in this approach.

form and style. In simple and general terms, the genre of a script or performance refers to the type of story being told, and the form and style refer to how the script is written and/or presented on stage. For example, a production could be of the southern gothic genre and surreal, abstract, fantastical or naturalistic in form and style. The choice of form has an impact on the choice of the world of the play and, consequently, what style of costume might be most suitable. This will then most likely have an influence on the style of drawing the designer applies, as argued above. Genre, form and style can mean different things, depending on what literature has been consulted and to what context these terms are applied. Sometimes these terms are used interchangeably. Apart from a few more thoughts in Chapter 3 on the subject, this book will not go deeper into this debate but will use these terms more loosely to benefit the focus of this book. Should there be an interest in studying theatre form and style in more depth, the

reader will be delighted to hear that there is an enormous amount of literature available.

The style of drawing is a result of various aspects, such as the quality of line, the medium used, the quality of contrast applied, the type of figurines and gestures used, and a specific colour combination or palette to name but a few. Some designers have developed a particular style of drawing due to the style of productions they tend to be involved in. The designer, and in fact any artist that draws or paints, develops, to varying degrees of abstraction, a set of symbols that refer to the real world. A drawing can never be the real thing; it attempts to convince the onlooker into accepting it as a substitute. The more abstract a drawing is, the more space there is for interpretation of what exactly its form represents. Drawing a character is a play with the onlooker. It is an experiment on how far removed a form can be from the real world and still be readable, convincing or, indeed, useful; this becomes a balancing act. It is creative, but

Costume illustrations by concept artist Phillip Boutté Jr. Left to right: *The Greatest Showman* (2017, directed by Michael Gracey, costume design by Ellen Mirojnick), *Once Upon A Time in Hollywood* (2019, directed by Quentin Tarantino, costume design by Arianne Phillips) and *Bohemian Rhapsody* (2018, directed by Bryan Singer, costume design by Julian Day).

also challenging, to determine what kind of mark a mouth, eye or hand, for example, can adopt in order to be recognized as such. The stick person is a good example, as it shows how little it takes to recognize the human figure. A series of marks will eventually make up something recognizable. Those marks tend to be unique to every designer and are the elements that determine their personal drawing style, which might still differ slightly from production to production. Developing a series of symbols representing the real thing, a shorthand so to speak, will undoubtedly be useful in developing a drawing style. It might be worth keeping the purpose of costume drawings in mind when developing this shorthand: they are, amongst other things, an instruction to the costume-maker. The designer can, of course, assist by answering questions, but a certain degree of detail might be appropriate. Alternatively, the designer might add a few technical drawings to the character drawing.

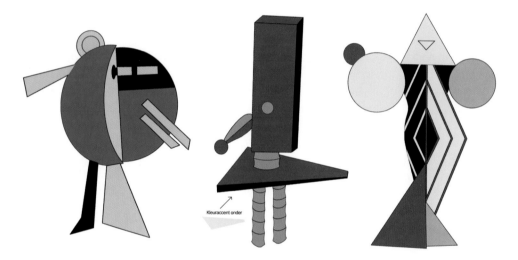

Costume designs can be much more abstract and less focused on the development of characters, as this costume design by wearable sculpture artist Daphne Karstens for *Het Grote Kleurenballet* (2019, by Rianne Meboer and Suzanne Bakker, directed by Anne van Dorp) demonstrates poignantly.

Realized costume designs by wearable sculpture artist Daphne Karstens for *Het Grote Kleurenballet* (2019, by Rianne Meboer and Suzanne Bakker, directed by Anne van Dorp, performers Tjebbe Roelofs, Suzanne Bakker and Rianne Meboer, sound design by Jolle Roelofs, stage and lighting design by Calle de Hoog, photographer Frank Wiersema).

Art Mediums Used by the Costume Designer

There is a great variety of different mediums and materials available to costume designers, which can be utilized to various effects. Watercolour paint, for example, has a very different visual effect to marker pens. Marker pens might lack the variety of shades that mixing watercolour can offer but are great to use when working away from the desk. Colour pencils might sometimes not reach the colour intensity that ink, for example, can achieve, but offer other advantages. Besides these more obvious reasons why a specific medium might be preferred, it may simply be habit or the way a medium feels when using it. With some mediums, it is possible to work very precisely, while others allow for a more generous stroke, such as pastels, crayons and chalk. It is also a good idea, when choosing the medium, to consider carefully the type and size of paper. When using pastels or colour pencils, for example, it is advisable to work on a larger format, whereas marker pens, or even watercolour, when used with a small brush, allow for working in smaller formats.

Watercolour

Watercolour paint is relatively easy to use, which makes it attractive when beginning to draw but it allows for the continued discovery and development of various techniques. It offers a great variety of shades and degrees of transparency. It consists of pigment and a binder, and the absence of any other substance leaves it transparent. It can achieve good colour vibrancy, but has its limitations. An attempt to achieve a high vibrancy or denser coverage could result in an undesirable muddy shade and damage to the paper. On that note, it is quite important to consider the choice of paper well, as this will have an effect on how many layers can be applied before it warps or even rips. It is quite remarkable what a difference a good quality paper makes when using watercolour paint.

An effective colour wash can be achieved using a big brush and plenty of water on high-quality watercolour paper. This can serve as a background or a first layer on to which details can be added. The wash is easy to accomplish but can have a great effect and always offers room for refinement and improvement.

Costume designs for *Romeo and Juliet* (1597, Shakespeare) by set and costume designer Bettina John (2014, a new dance adaptation with Avant Garde Dance by Tony Adigun and Maxwell Golden).

Costume designs for *Romeo and Juliet*.

Watercolour is available in liquid form filled into tubes or as solid cubes available individually or as a set. As opposed to acrylic or oil paint, watercolour does not harden permanently and can be rewetted. That means brushes are less likely to harden when left uncleaned. It also means paint can be left to dry and re-activated with water, as well as removed, depending on the surface. A set of twelve colours is plenty to start with, but much larger sets and a great range of colours is available. There is a vast variety of brushes available and, roughly speaking, it comes down to trying them. A cheaper brush does not need to suggest less good results, but the wrong brush might make the process more difficult. There are brushes that are suitable for acrylic, which mostly can be used for oil too, and then those suitable to use with watercolour. Watercolour works well in combination with almost any other medium.

GOUACHE

Gouache, sometimes also referred to as opaque watercolour paint, is widely used among commercial artists, such as designers and illustrators, and is much loved for its particular features, such as its colour intensity and opaque quality. As opposed to watercolour paint, gouache has an additional, chalk-like ingredient that makes the paint more likely to appear opaque. It is easy to use, particularly because, like watercolour, it can be rewetted, making its use much less wasteful. It is mainly offered in tubes, which, like watercolour, will last for a while. Both can be used in combination and, in fact, share many qualities, but differ in that watercolour is transparent and gouache semi- or fully opaque. That means gouache can achieve deeper hues and it can be layered without the underneath layer necessarily showing. That can be particularly helpful when wanting to add white reflections, for example, on to a finished costume drawing,

Costume designs by set and costume designer Jerome Bourdin for the characters Myriam and Palema of the novel *Du Vent Dans Les Branches De Sassafras* (1966, René Obaldia), using gouache. Although these drawings have been created on paper, the designer photographed them in order to touch them up digitally using Photoshop, a common workflow amongst designers today.

which can be extremely effective in this context. Both paints dry very fast compared to oil or acrylic paints, making layering very easy and drawing a fairly fast business, which, as a designer, is a quality very much to be appreciated. When considering which of the two to use, it is really a question as to whether the opaque or transparent quality is preferred. If both of these qualities could be useful, then a combination of the two mediums might be the best choice.

Colour Pencils and Water-Soluble Pencils

Colour pencils are a great addition to the above-mentioned paints. Although effective on their own, mixed with paint they can help to achieve more effects. Due to their response to water,

water-soluble or watercolour pencils allow for a wider range of effects, compared to the standard colour pencil. They work well in combination with watercolour paint, particularly when wanting to add details like hair, eyes or the texture of a particular material, such as pin-stripe wool. They are often sold in large sets of up to a hundred pencils, offering a wide range of colour shades and making it a cost-effective option. A watercolour wash in combination with an added colour pencil line, drawn into slightly wet paper, can not only have a great effect, but can be an inspiring exercise at the beginning stages of drawing. A blank piece of paper will always be a challenging way to start; however, a paper with a beautiful wash on it can do wonders to the searching mind of the designer.

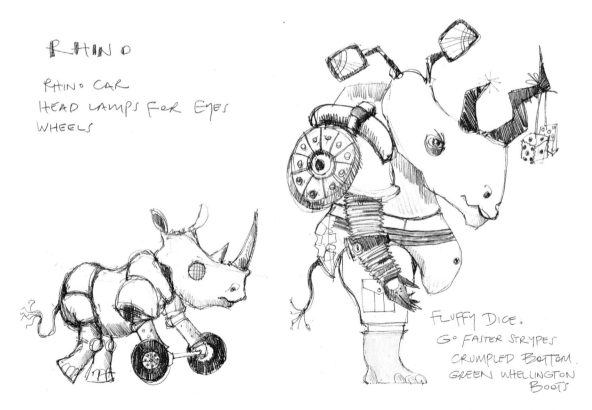

Many designers use colour pencils in combination with other media. This picture shows a costume design by set and costume designer Jason Southgate for *James and the Giant Peach* (2007, Citizens Theatre, directed by Jeremy Raison), using pencil and colour pencils.

PASTELS

Pastels are not as widely used for costume drawing amongst designers, as they do not allow for enough details. However, that does not mean pastels cannot be useful or even preferable in some instances, for example, for life-drawing and other studies, especially on larger scale formats. They allow for the exploration of bigger forms, the bigger picture and the design elements such as colour palette, silhouette and composition. They can be especially useful when the tendency persists to focus in on detail and there is a risk of losing sight of the overall feel for the design. Pastels could be useful in collages, being effective even when applied on to magazine cut-outs and coloured paper.

INK

Ink, for the purpose of drawing, is mostly used in liquid form. This particular form is called drawing ink. However, ink is also available in the form of powder or paste and widely used for printing, such as screen-printing. Being one of the oldest, if not the oldest, painting medium, there are now many different types of inks, but the one most useful to designers is the one sold in the form of an aqueous solution, filled into small tubs. As opposed to watercolour and gouache paint, drawing ink is already liquid enough to be used instantly, allowing for an even distribution of pigment on the paper and achieving incredible vibrancy without the need of layering. Similar to watercolour paint, with the help of a reasonably thick brush it can create a beautiful wash on paper. Alternatively, it can be applied using a nib, allowing for a very thin and precise line. Ink is probably one of the most versatile mediums, available in many shapes and forms.

Costume design ideas for dance by set and costume designer Frankie Bradshaw. Although created in the digital drawing program *Procreate*, this drawing shows the effect of pastels very well and the potential of digital drawing tools to realistically recreate the effect of a great variety of art mediums.

Costume illustrations by costume designer Maryna Gradnova using ink.

MARKER PENS

A rather modern way of drawing, compared to the above mediums, marker pens are very popular amongst fashion designers and have, in recent years, seen an increased popularity amongst costume designers too. The absence of water makes markers a lot less messy and simpler to use. Especially when travelling, having a pack of markers handy seems a lot easier than paint, brushes and water, not to mention saving the cleaning of it all afterwards. Every brand has slightly different qualities and can vary greatly, sometimes frustratingly so, in their colour and shade. The range of markers is ever expanding, developing various different extra features, such as softer, brush-like tips, which allows for a lot more flexibility in the mark-making. Most markers have two tips: a thick and a thin one. Some brands offer a blender pen, which eases the blending of colours; it works to a limited degree and the paper plays a crucial role in the success of this technique. The market offers paper known as marker or graphic paper, on which it is easier to use the pen. Instead of absorbing the pigment, it sits on top of the surface, allowing for a more vibrant colour. The paint stays moist just that little bit longer, easing the blending technique. At first, markers appear very easy to use but, in fact, are quite tricky to master, as they are more limited than watercolour paint, for example. While, with a little bit of practice, mixing watercolour paint will achieve any desired shade of colour, marker pens can only offer the shades they come in and those that are available to the designer in that moment. As mentioned, blending them is limited. These are reasons why designers use marker pens in combination with other mediums, such as watercolour paint.

Using watercolour or gouache paint can be a more intuitive experience, whereas the marker pens require more concentration when choosing the right shade, and once the marker pen is applied, there is no way back. Layering watercolour allows for more flexibility when exploring desired colours. However, the effect of markers can be striking, and an attractive graphic effect can be achieved. It is important to be aware that

Costume design by Ysa Dora Abba for Oscar Wilde's *The Importance of Being Earnest* (1985), created as part of the UAL Costume Design for Performance short course, 2019. The drawings are created using *Promarker* pens and colour pencils in combination.

Costume design by costume designer Sophie Ruth Donaldson for *Stunners* (2019, Tamar & Jo). The drawings are created using *Promarker* pens and pencils in combination.

marker pens dry out relatively quickly, especially in a hot climate, and storing them in a cool place, away from sunshine, will extend their lifespan dramatically.

White Ink Pens

The type of ink used to make ink pens is very thick and not water-soluble, it is water-resistant. Their composition makes them extremely opaque, allowing their paint to sit on top of any kind of medium, which is why they enjoy such popularity. No matter what medium is used in a drawing, one of these pens will work on top of it, allowing the addition of details, such as patterns, lace, sparkles and reflections. They come in a great variety of shapes offered by various brands, some of them with fine metal tips and others with thicker felt tips.

This drawing, by designer Laura Belzin, demonstrates how the white ink pen can be used to create texture, specifically lace; created as part of the UAL Costume Design for Performance course, 2019.

LADY BRACKNELL

Costume design by designer Laura Belzin for *The Importance of Being Earnest (1985, Oscar Wilde)*, as part of the UAL Costume Design for Performance course, 2019.

DIGITAL DRAWING SOFTWARE

Digital drawing is an exciting new field. It is progressing incredibly fast, offering new tools frequently. When considering which digital drawing tools to get, the number of options available can be overwhelming or at least a little confusing. When one tool has been hailed the best option a year ago, the chances that this is still the case are slim, although most people would not even know. It is more important for the designer to find the tool that works for them, rather than trying to keep up with all the new releases. In the last decade, a lot of designers have relied on a digital tablet that connects to a computer, similarly to a mouse. The tablet ordinarily comes with a digital drawing pen, some of which offer a wide range of tips. However, the separation of the eyes–the display–the hands–the tablet has been only partially satisfactory. Something had been missing and when the 'display tablet' became more readily available, a lot of professionals embraced the latter, overwhelmingly stating that it was a more intuitive tool and achieved better results when trying to hand-draw. It simply comes closer to the natural way of drawing.

Roughly speaking, 'display tablets' divide into two versions. One version is a computer in its own right and comes with its own software. This might be a disadvantage for those who have an established digital workflow with software such as Photoshop or Affinity. However, others might feel comfortable working with the software that is available for their tablet. The other display tablet version needs connecting to a computer or phone and, consequently, functions as a second monitor, allowing for the continued use of software installed on the computer. This tablet is dependent on a computer to work, which could be a disadvantage for some designers. For example, if a designer wants to make use of digital drawing tools whilst travelling, needing an additional computer might

feel cumbersome and slightly defeats the point. The cost for display tablets can be pretty substantial, depending on the quality of the display and/ or monitor. However, there are great affordable options available on the market.

Any digital tool will come with a certain price. Looking at the constant need to update and upgrade to newer software and computers implies that this cost will persist. It is important to be aware of any future costs and worthwhile to consider various options. For some designers, that might mean paying a monthly subscription fee to allow access to software; for other designers, that might mean purchasing a tablet with software already installed. Some of the most popular suppliers of digital drawing equipment have been the Wacom tablet range and the iPad with its Apple Pen solution. Additional to the hardware, there is a range of digital drawing software available, some of which can only be used with certain devices. One of the most popular and cost-effective solutions seems

Costume illustrations by concept artist Phillip Boutté Jr for *Black Panther* (2018, directed by Ryan Coogler, costume design by Ruth E Carter), created digitally.

Costume designs by set and costume designer Adam Nee. Left to right: *Priscilla Queen of the Desert* (2006, Stephan Elliott, Allan Scott), the novel *The Lady of the Camellias* (1852, Alexandre Dumas) adapted as a ballet and *Richard III* (1633, William Shakespeare), all created digitally, using a variety of techniques in Photoshop. Note the very successful combination of digital drawing and photo-collaging.

to be a software called 'Procreate', which can be used in combination with the iPad. It is not only incredibly intuitive, but also compact and practical, especially compared to other digital drawing tools. While it is still a substantial cost, it seems, to a lot of designers, worth it.

Digital tools are incredibly useful and can speed up the workflow, while achieving compelling new aesthetics. Incorporating new technology into a workflow often means achieving new results. Digital drawing has changed the way designers work and their results tremendously. For example, there is the option to zoom into a drawing, which allows for more accuracy or to duplicate elements and place them into a drawing as many times as desired. Working with layers can be enormously useful, when trying out different colour combinations, for example. Layers can simply be turned on and off, as well as allowing for changes to their opacity. Costume designers can import any texture or fabric and work it into their costume design. However, this needs a bit of practising, and getting the proportion right is crucial.

This development does not mean more traditional methods and mediums are less valid. Both options have their advantages and disadvantages, and a combination of both new and old technologies, has a lot of potential. Hybrid visualization, for example, particularly popular amongst architects, is developing steadily. To create hybrid visualizations, designers and architects use digital tools, often to speed up the process or to achieve an effect more challenging when done with traditional tools and to add a hand-drawn element to it. This approach is a promising direction for costume designers too. It allows digital drawings to appear less synthetic, a disadvantage often heard of in relation to using digital drawing.

Drawing Fabrics and Other Materials

The following sections will lay out the main principles to keep in mind when illustrating fabric in a costume drawing. Doing so effectively requires a bit of practice but is worthwhile spending time on. New drawing technologies, such as Photoshop and Procreate, might be helpful but, equally, they will require learning and practising. Before going into it, it needs to be said that there is no right or wrong way. All that matters is whether the designer is able to communicate their design vision to the rest of the production team successfully. And, even if the designer's drawing is very accomplished, the fabric swatch, next to the costume drawing, is often required to reduce misinterpretations, especially regarding the exact colour and texture of the fabric. No matter how successful the drawing is, it will always leave some uncertainty about the exact fabric intended for the costume. Continuous liaising with the costume team is crucial. However, developing the skill to draw fabric effectively is desirable for various reasons. To mention but a few, first of all, the drawing will be better and more convincing. A convincing drawing makes it more likely for the designer to gain respect. It makes communication much easier, especially when the designer is not available at all times. Second, there is not always the right fabric swatch available at the time of designing the costumes. Third, the designer might want to consult with a costume-maker about the exact fabric and discuss options over a well-drawn costume illustration that gives clear ideas of drape and weight of the desired fabric. More information on the fabric choice itself can be found in Chapter 3.

Light

Learning how to draw fabrics and materials starts with developing the habit to observe carefully and to study their qualities. In fact, this is fundamental to learning how to draw, generally. First and foremost, in order to draw materials, it is crucial to understand how materials respond to light, reflect it and absorb it. Different materials respond to light in different ways, which allows for information about its qualities to be obtained and, consequently, a judgement on what kind of material it is. When wanting to simulate silk in a drawing, for example, it is important to understand the way it reflects light. In comparison to wool, silk reflects light a lot more, whereas wool barely does and, therefore, appears matt. The stronger the contrast between light and shadow, the shinier a material will appear. It is good to be aware of this effect and to use it when wanting to achieve a particular quality that then allows for judgements of character and context. For example, subtly shiny fabric tends to appear luxurious but very shiny fabric is much showier or even tacky. In cases where wool has a slight shimmer to it, it will, most likely, consist of several materials, such as cashmere or silk. Deciding to give a wool suit a slight shimmer in their costume drawing, which will make it appear more expensive, the designer might intend the character to appear richer. However, when adding a lot of shine to it, it could easily appear a little tacky, implying the use of cheaper materials, such as a low-quality polyester mix.

Drape

The second quality to consider when drawing fabric is its drape. Simulating the fabric's drape and its response to light successfully in a drawing allows the onlooker to read it correctly. How rigid or soft a material is will determine the mark-making and stroke that needs to be applied when intending to draw it. A garment made of rigid material, like cotton drill, for example, has a crisp and clear silhouette, which needs to be simulated in the drawing to indicate this material. Its creases need to have the same quality of rigidness. A softer material, such as velvet, on the other hand, will show softer lines around the creases and a softer transition between light and shade, but will, interestingly, still have quite a structured silhouette when used for a blazer, for example. The mark-making in a drawing needs to be adapted to these qualities, resulting in either a fine or strong line and a straight or rather squiggly line.

Costume designs by set and costume designer Jerome Bourdin for Leila of the opera *Les Pêcheurs de Perles* (1863, Georges Bizet). Bourdin used gouache to add highlights and achieve a transparent appearing veil.

Jersey, for example, is a relatively heavy material and, therefore, gravitates toward the floor. It has some stretch to it, hence behaving less stiffly and more fluidly. Jersey tends to cling around the body, hence exposing its shape. Depending on the jersey's composition and weight, it is less prone to crease. Considering these qualities in a drawing will result in the correct reading of the fabric. Cotton tends to be a bit stiffer, keeping the garment's own shape as opposed to clinging to the body. Silk taffeta is a very rigid material, barely losing its shape when worn and barely exposing the body. Drawing a garment made of such materials needs to only show the shape of the garment itself, rather than also showing the body underneath.

Stiffer materials tend to crease a lot more, which can be incorporated in the drawing, helping to understand it better. Stiff fabrics also require a precise pattern in order to sit tightly on the body. Garments constructed in this way appear more structured than a T-shirt or jersey dress, for example. This can be reflected in crisper lines. Similar-appearing fabrics, such as organza and chiffon, both lightweight and semi-transparent fabrics, can also be distinguished by the way they drape. Chiffon, particularly when made of silk, is very

Costume designs by set and costume designer Jerome Bourdin for the opera *Lakmé* (1883, Léo Delibes). Bourdin used Gouache to add highlights and achieve a transparent appearing veil.

flowy, while organza has a stiffer drape. Again, the line can help to indicate the correct fabric in this case. Furthermore, in the case of transparency, the body needs to be shown underneath, as laid out in the next section.

TRANSPARENCY

Another quality that allows for the judgement of materials in a drawing is the use of transparency. Chiffon, organdie, clear plastic, netting or fine cottons are, to varying degrees, transparent. In order to simulate a specific type of transparent fabric in a drawing successfully, the focus needs to be on the layer underneath and how it appears with the transparent fabric on top. In most cases, it is the body that will be visible. Some materials, such as muslin, will let the layer underneath come through a little bit, whereas a material like clear plastic leaves what is underneath in full sight. It is important to keep in mind the lighting state of the performance, as every material responds to light in a different way, which is what makes a fabric unique and identifiable. Some materials appear transparent only when seen against light, others will appear more opaque under certain lighting conditions. While some circumstances can barely be predicted, a lot of knowledge on how materials respond to light is available or easily obtainable by testing. For example, simply shining light on to a fabric sample, using a torch or lamp, is a way to find out how a certain fabric responds to light. When using a variety of very different fabrics in a production, it is good to know whether any of them stands out more. In this case, all fabrics in question could be placed next to each other and lit with a small lamp. Simulating a costume in a drawing, as close to reality as possible, with the knowledge achieved through experimentation, for example, is a pretty good way of understanding whether it will work as intended.

TEXTURE

Using texture is probably the most enjoyable part of drawing materials, as it can be hugely effective in illustrating it. A lot of fabrics came to have a particular kind of texture because of the way they are produced and the material used. The most significant factors on how a texture appears are the warp and the weft threads, the two opposing threads woven together in the process of fabric weaving and how they are woven together. Cotton drill, for example, is made of thick cotton threads, woven together in a way to achieve a strong and resilient material, resulting in a very noticeable texture. Finer materials, such as chiffon or organza, barely have any texture. Organza is a plain weave fabric that barely accounts for any space between two weaving threads in the weft and in the warp, hence appearing much less textured. Organza and tulle, for example, are both lightweight and see-through, but their structure and, therefore, their texture are very different. A closer look reveals that tulle is like netting and resembles a hexagonal mesh, resulting in a much more noticeable texture. When drawing less-textured materials, other qualities such as its drape and transparency need to be captured in order to simulate them successfully in a drawing. Most wools, for example, have a strong texture and capturing this in the drawing will help to make it identifiable as wool. The weaving and knitting processes not only produce fabric with a certain texture, but also a pattern, which is often deliberately designed, as is the case with jacquard fabric, such as brocade, damask or Marseille's cloth. Furthermore, texture can be achieved by a pattern printed on to a fabric. The appearance of a printed pattern, as well as any other texture, greatly depends on the distance from which it is seen. The designer needs to be aware of the effect a certain distance will have on the designs.

SPECIAL MATERIALS

Fur, feathers, sequins, metal studs and other unusual materials can be very exciting as part of a costume design and are enjoyable to add to a drawing – and indeed to the costume itself, particularly to add texture. It is important to observe and then capture the essence of a particular material, possibly their main element, and find an effective shorthand that can stand in for it in a drawing.

Costume design by set and costume designer Jerome Bourdin for a stage adaptation of *Chitty Chitty Bang Bang* (1968, musical adventure fantasy film, written by Irwin Kostal and Roald Dahl). Bourdin used gouache to create texture and highlights on top of the darker shades as well as touching the drawings up digitally.

Sometimes this shorthand or symbol can be far removed from reality but that does not matter, as long as it works and translates as such in the drawing. Fur, for example, will never have as sharp an outline as clear plastic or a tailored suit. Hence the outline of a garment made of fur needs to be more broken up, softer and livelier to achieve the right appearance in the drawing. One of the recommended exercises at the end of this chapter is to draw details and close-ups of various materials. This is a vital, regular practice for understanding and learning how to approach more complex materials.

Capturing in a drawing a unique combination of qualities, such as light, drape, texture and transparency, allows for a pretty precise judgement of the type of material and kind of fabric the designer wishes to achieve. It is the unique combination of those qualities that make fabric appear the way it does. It is important not to forget that anything in a costume drawing will be read and understood by the onlooker in a certain way and the ideal scenario is that this is in line with the intention of the designer. In other words, ideally, the designer is in full control of their mark-making, always being aware of what the line is referring to in reality. On the way of becoming an accomplished illustrator, the designer, absolutely, can give supportive information, such as fabric and colour swatches, notes and verbal communication. Some designers even choose to rely more on supportive information than the costume drawing.

EXERCISES

Exercise 1: Tracing Silhouettes

Make a selection of references you found of fashion plates or photographs for a period play of your choice and interest, and trace them by either using tracing paper or a lighting box. Holding the reference and a white piece of paper against the window can also be an effective method to trace a silhouette but a lighting box is not available. Include not only dresses and suits, but also shoes, hair and accessories. Avoid getting too hung up with all the historical accuracy at this point. You can come back to this later, or you might not need to. This is a good practice for improving the drawing of figurines, clothing and drape, and helps understanding of the key elements of period costume.

Exercise 2: Creating a Collage

Take a script you are already familiar with and choose one character to focus on for this exercise. After having conducted relevant research on the play and the chosen character, start collecting materials that seem relevant to the character. This could be in relation to colour, texture, fabrics, shapes or mood and should happen in a more intuitive manner at this stage. Start cutting and assembling your materials on an A3-sized piece of paper. You can also look for relevant material online or in your digital research, and print some of it out. The same exercise can be repeated for other characters of your chosen play. It is worth following the advice given in this exercise and produce a hard copy of the collage, rather than rely on digital tools only. Moving on to a digital version can be done at a later stage.

Exercise 3: Practice Figure Drawing

Life-drawing does not necessarily need to mean drawing people without clothes, although joining a regular life-drawing class, where this is the case, is very useful for practising your drawing skills and for learning more about the body and how it moves. For this exercise, however, you only need to find a volunteer who agrees to let you draw them in the clothes of their or, if possible, your choice. If they are comfortable with it, ask them to position themselves in various different ways. You do not need to spend a long time on each drawing. Try and grasp the essence of the posture and how the clothes respond to it specifically. Experiment with different garments, such as a skirt, a blouse, trousers and shorts, and look at various cuts and styles. You could try and resemble the period you are interested in with the choice of clothes, your wardrobe permitting. You could take pictures of several poses to use at a later stage.

Exercise 4: Observing People

A costume tells a story but the clothes a person wears tells a story too. Observing what people wear and how they wear it is an almost essential exercise for a costume designer. A costume designer will do this without really thinking about it. It will have become a reflex and is a form of studying. Try it! Go to a public space where you can sit down and watch people. Choose a person that you find interesting and that you can observe for a while, without being obtrusive. Have a notebook ready. Think about that person. Where are they headed? Do they live here or are they on a holiday? What does their home look like? What interests do they have? Where do they shop? Do they have a partner or children? Do they have a pet? Find your own questions relevant to the person you choose and write down your answers. Those can be keywords, or you can attempt to write a little story or poem about the person you encountered. Depending on the time you spent on one, choose a couple more and repeat the exercise. In between, think about the reasons why you have come to those conclusions about the person and make notes. As an alternative, you can find a picture of a person unbeknownst to you and conduct the same exercise.

Exercise 5: Drawing Faces

Drawing faces can be a challenge but to develop a character and complete it by adding a face to your drawing is very much advisable. The challenge is to overcome the fear that the attempt to draw the face will not be successful, but without trying, there cannot be an improvement. The answer to this problem is to practise and gain confidence. Take a piece of paper and draw at least ten shapes that resemble an oval or circle. They do not have to be perfect and should all differ slightly. Now start making marks in place of the eyes, nose and mouth. Experiment with different mark-making. Start small and then try bigger marks. Observe the effect and respond to your observations in the next attempt. Repeat this exercise as much as necessary over the course of a few weeks or months.

Exercise 6: Experimenting with Different Mediums

Have watercolour paint, plenty of water, a big brush and various types of paper ready. Collect paper from various sources and recycle where possible. Using plenty of water, choose a colour and make a generous mark on the paper of your choice. This is called a wash and can be used as a

background for a figurine or a rough outline of the figurine itself. Washes can be very effective and a great inspiration for a following drawing. Repeat this exercise with varying amounts of water and on different types of paper. Observe the effects and elaborate on your findings. Repeat this exercise with gouache and with other types of paint that you have available, and study the different effects. At a later stage, you can start drawing into the wet wash with a water-soluble pencil. Observe the results.

Exercise 7: Experimenting with Texture

Prepare a piece of paper with ten to twenty squares, all of the same size. Using a pencil, experiment with different marks, such as dots, small lines, longer lines, thick lines, narrow lines and vary their distance. Use soft pencils as well as harder ones. You can try making vertical marks, horizontal ones or diagonal ones. Observe the effect. See if any of your squares resemble a material that you know or that is around you. Have a think about which of the textures that you have created could be useful when trying to depict a particular fabric in a costume drawing. The next step of this exercise is to use an actual material as a starting point and try to re-create its texture in the prepared squares.

Exercise 8: Drawing Materials

As mentioned earlier in this chapter, observing the drape and light-reflection properties of textiles is vital for understanding how to draw them. For this exercise, collect several different fabrics and materials or objects made of fabric. You could use your own clothes, soft furnishings around you, such as a blanket, curtains or actual fabric pieces. Make sure they are of a decent size, so that you can drape them on the table, over a chair or another object. You need to arrange them in a way to allow for a drape to occur so that you can observe how the light hits its surface in different ways. Observe how much contrast occurs between the various shades and what role the texture plays. Draw a variety of textiles in this way using pencil, charcoal, pastels, watercolour or gouache. Observe which medium is most useful in translating a particular texture or material.

Exercise 9: Matching Colour

Prepare a piece of paper drawing out ten to twenty squares all of the same size. Have watercolours, water and brushes ready. In the first square, try and match your exact skin colour by mixing the colours available to you. Repeat this exercise for the remaining squares, using skin colours of your friends and family or, alternatively, use photographs.

Observe the fine nuances in colour. Once you have re-created a good variety of skin colours, start with a new piece of paper and try matching the colours of clothes and objects around you.

Exercise 10: Drawing an Ageing Garment

Choose a type a garment, such as a shirt. Prepare this exercise by drawing a simplified version of it several times on to the same page, just like a technical drawing or a thumbnail. Start working on the first drawing, making it appear new and crisp. Every following drawing is a step further toward an aged version of this garment. Think about how the outline of the garment might change, how its colour is affected, whether it will have any rips, holes or stains and where those are likely to appear first.

3
FUNDAMENTAL DESIGN CONSIDERATIONS

PARAMETERS AND HOW TO NAVIGATE THEM

The Brief

The first incentive for a costume design, apart from the script, of course, comes from the brief, which can come in as many forms as there are productions. A brief can be an email sent to a designer or their agent by a producer or a director asking the designer if they want to get involved in a production. A brief could also simply be communicated in a short conversation between the designer and the director, in person, over the phone or, spontaneously, at a networking event, for example. A brief can be very detailed or consist of only a few rough ideas. It can be surprisingly informal. Some briefs are flexible, others, or at least aspects of it, non-negotiable. In many cases, the brief is already partly defined by the company producing the show. Some director/designer teams have worked together for a while and have developed an aesthetic and an understanding through their many conversations and joint interests and experiences. In this instance, a brief may not be required any more. On the other hand, in the beginning of a work relationship, more in-depth conversations need to happen. When applying for a designer role on a production, the brief often is included in

the advertisement of the role, giving the designer a chance to decide if they want it and to determine whether they are the best candidate for it. Additionally, the designer might want to investigate the people involved, look at their work, their style and track record. The designer is well advised to determine whether the brief works for them, whether they have the skills and resources and, very importantly, investigate which part of the brief is flexible. Some aspects of a brief might appear rigid but with a good idea and good persuasion skills, a designer is well able to steer a production more toward their liking and skill-set, as long as the play allows for it.

Most briefs contain the name of the production, the production company, the name of the director and other creatives involved, the venue, whether a tour is planned and, if so, an idea of the various locations and, possibly, a short synopsis of the script. It will give the designer an idea of the timeframe, including the opening date and time, and how many performances are planned to take place. It might also give an idea of fees and budget. Additionally, there could be information on the style and form the production team and director are aiming for and sometimes additional thoughts on what they are looking for in a designer and the design. If any of this information is not included, a little bit of investigating will surely lead to answers. It might be the case that the designer already has some of the information from having worked with the team before, for example. Last but not least, it could be the case that parts of the brief are negotiable, flexible or subject to change. As mentioned earlier, the designer will have to contemplate whether or not they want to accept a job and the brief is the first opportunity to do so. It is also the starting point for the research and for finding ideas.

The Designer's Personal Interests, Style and Experience

A designer's personal interests, their experience and personal style play a major role in the direction a costume design takes. These are the designer's evolving and ever-growing assets, and, therefore, often the reason why they have been asked to get involved in a production. When a producer or director chooses a designer specifically based on their style, which is very often the case, aspects of the design brief become secondary, as they were already negotiated when the choice of the designer was being made. Fashion designers and artists, are often asked to design for opera or dance because of their unique style. In these cases, the producer is particularly interested in their personal response to the play, story

Costume drawings can vary in style dramatically, as these examples by designer and visual dramaturge Brad Caleb Lee (left) and costume designer Sophie Ruth Donaldson (right) demonstrate well. The style should depend on the production and an attempt to reflect it should be made. Both examples are for very different productions, stylistically as well as in form and genre. Left: *Out of Darkness* (2016/18, opera, composer Jake Heggie, librettist Gene Scheer) and right: *Impending: Head to head, Head to Bum, Crotch to Crotch* (2019, Florence Peake and Eve Stainton).

or subject in question. Certain genres or forms of the performing arts, such as contemporary dance and modern opera, are more conducive to a designer who wants to explore their personal interests and develop their style. Opera directors and choreographers tend to invite experimental design approaches. This offers the designer the chance to develop an idea they have had for a while. Having a style can help a designer to get offered more work of a particular kind that suits their style, which tends to be closely linked to personal interests. Equally, it can be limiting to have a very distinct style in terms of the type of work that will be offered.

Genre

Genre can be a confusing term. It is sometimes used to refer to the different forms and/or industries of the performing arts, such as film, television and theatre, as well as the various forms within them, such as opera, dance, music theatre, short film or documentary. Within these, there are various genres and/or forms, such as political and naturalistic theatre, baroque and modern opera, contemporary dance, ballet or rock ballet and many cross-overs. The meaning of these terms can overlap greatly and depends on the context and perspective of the literature or conversation.

Costume drawing by set and costume designer Nicky Shaw for *La Cenerentola* (1817, opera by Rossini).

Every genre has its own conventions attached to it, be it comedy or tragedy, musical theatre or political theatre, modern opera or contemporary dance, or the many film-specific genres, such as science fiction, adventure or horror. The designer is well advised to be aware of these conventions and to take them into account when considering getting involved in a production and starting to explore design ideas. While the visual conventions are often more prevalent, conventions extend to the approach to storytelling and the text itself. In fact, conventions are often derived from the text, which then has an impact on the visual language, the style and form of a performance or film.

The development of the production of a theatre play, for example, can be very character- and text-based. A good understanding of literature and how to analyse scripts is useful here to help delve into the characters and be able to have in-depth conversations about the text and its themes and concepts. Often the first step in the design process is to establish the time period and location of the setting and the relationships between the characters. A social drama theatre play, such as *Sing Yer Heart Out for the Lads* (2002, Roy Williams) allows the costume designer to develop realistic characters and to make subtle design choices, which can make or break the production. The focus here

Costume illustrations for film by concept artist Phillip Boutté Jr. Left: Supreme Intelligence of *Captain Marvel* (2019, directed by Anna Boden and Ryan Fleck, costume design by Sanja Milkovic Hays). Right: Mrs Who of *Wrinkle in Time* (2018, directed by Ava DuVernay, costume design by Paco Delgado).

will be on rendering believable characters and, by doing so, supporting the message of the play. A children's play, on the other hand, might be an opportunity to have a more experimental-design approach.

A dance production often does not use text at all. It might have a narrative at its core. It might use a story, script or text of some other kind, such as a poem or novel, as a starting point, but then translates this into a more abstract form. A dance piece might be developed from themes and concepts only. Some productions might centre around music. A ballet will often have a narrative and music as its guiding factors. Contemporary dance is often more abstract and discussions around concept and movement are more prevalent. A contemporary dance piece has more room for abstract ideas and unusual design solutions. Some understanding of different movement styles and the influential work of certain choreographers will be beneficial in understanding what a choreographer is trying to communicate through their choreography. Often the first step for the choreographer and the designer is to establish the movement language, themes and how the audience should respond to the piece.

In order to optimize the collaboration with performance artists, some knowledge of art

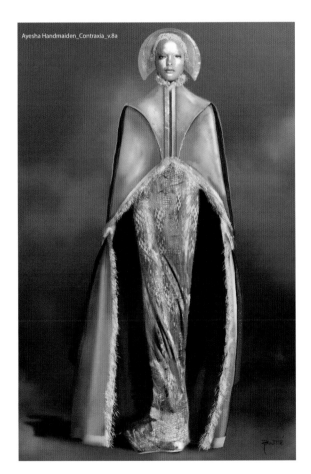

Costume illustrations for film by concept artist Phillip Boutté Jr. Left: Ayesha Handmaiden of *Guardians of the Galaxy 2* (2017, directed by James Gunn, costume design by Judianna Makovsky). Right: Sharon Tate of *Once Upon A Time in Hollywood* (2019, directed by Quentin Tarantino, costume design by Arianne Phillips).

and contemporary culture will help to support or to elevate their performance through the costume design.

Opera and musical productions are often more stylized than theatre and most film productions. Their design approach tends to be exaggerated and symbolic. Having some understanding of music and the different types of opera will help to understand the structure and traditional approaches. Early discussions are often around the style of music and drama in the various scenes and the stylization of the characters. On a side note, it is worth pointing out that, throughout this process, it is important that the designer and the creative team are mindful regarding any stereotyping.

Some genre aesthetics can be very strong, such as science-fiction films, or they can be more subtle, such as contemporary social drama. A horror film, for example, will most certainly, at some point, introduce surreal moments and give the costume designer a chance to create some fantastical costumes. A coming-of-age feature film, such as *The Breakfast Club* (1985, directed by John Hughes, costume design by Marylin Vance), gives a costume designer the chance to explore current social behaviour and fashion. Historical films and dramas, such as *Call the Midwife* or *The Crown*, give a costume designer the opportunity to do profound research on historical costumes; they require, more than anything, a great interest in period costume and its accuracy. When working on a historical film, portraying figures such as Elizabeth I or a drama such as *Schindler's List* (1993, Steven Spielberg), the designer will be required to do more research on period costume. The production time on such films can be far longer than a theatre play, due to the sheer amount of research that goes into it or, indeed, the making of the many costumes for the crowd scenes alone.

The overall premise remains to serve the script, if there is one. The respective conventions of a genre are a starting point and cannot simply be ignored; however, both script and genre can be challenged by the creative team. They can decide to work with the script and genre conventions or against it, exaggerate it, mock it or play with it, but there will be a limit to how far it can be challenged. An interest in the subject matter, an understanding of the story and the desire and skill to tell it through costume will be necessary to deliver a good design in any genre. Some designers love the research aspect to historical dramas; others need the freer approach of modern opera, for example, to feel fulfilled. A designer is well advised to listen to their inner voice and follow the work they enjoy and are good at.

Form and Style

Theatre and film can take a variety of different forms, from naturalistic, also often referred to as realistic, to much more experimental. A fundamental decision over form and style of a production will have to be made prior to any design conversations, as this will set out the basic rules for the production in general and, consequently, the design. Those decisions will have been made early on, either by the producer, production company, the director or choreographer. By inviting companies with an experimental approach to theatre, for example, the artistic director or producer is inviting the pushing of boundaries of what theatre means; this will inevitably extend to ideas of design, costume and clothing. The reader might find that studying examples of experimental theatre, dance and film could be insightful in understanding the impact that style and form have on design choices.

A lot of the time, form is determined by the script or the choice of the script and the genre it can be subscribed to. Scripts, written in a particular way, abstract texts or text fragments, for example, but also naturalistic storytelling, demand a particular form that can hardly be ignored. Some professionals, dramaturgs, for example, have the expertise to change scripts and give them a different form or allow for the script to take a new form. Good producers and artistic directors have a clear idea of the form and style they want their productions to be in and will approach a director and designer or company that can deliver that. A producer might want a traditional form of theatre or a more experimental approach, which in turn will impact costume design options. This is the first instance where decisions over the design have been made without the designer necessarily being involved.

The form of naturalistic theatre, for example, demands a realistic representation of life in the time the script is set. The design needs to follow the rules of the naturalistic world of the play. Whether set in a particular period or in contemporary times, naturalistic costumes need to represent real people in a convincing way. That often means costumes draw less attention to themselves and support the realistic portrayal of the character. Other forms of theatre might allow for costumes to take centre stage, a children's play, for example, a story such as *Alice in Wonderland*. If the creative team decides to inject surreal moments, fantastical sequences or science-fiction scenarios, the costume design will have to reflect this. The more experimental and unconventional the creative team is with their approach to form, the more unconventional the costume design can be. Answers to what is possible lie in the logic of the world constructed in conversations between members of the creative team.

The Designer–Director Relationship

As mentioned in the sections above, some of the design parameters might already be set out by choosing to work with a particular director known to have a particular style. The relationship between the designer and director plays a key role in a production and the nature of this relationship can vary greatly. One important factor is the way a production team has been formed and who the initiator was. In many cases, the team, which is brought together for a production, has not previously worked together or even known each other before. In those cases, the designer and director have to work a little bit harder to get to know each other, build up trust and develop a language together. Most of the time, especially in those scenarios, the director assumes the role of the leader who brings the team together and makes the final decisions. This is widely accepted as the norm, but it does not need to be this way and other members of the team could assume this role or share it.

It is common for directors and designers to go on a creative journey and build on their joint experience over the course of several productions, which can result in a strong common language. This can impact the position of the designer and their influence. In a familiar relationship, the director might be much more open to discuss fundamental

Collages by costume designer Sophie Ruth Donaldson for *Stunners* (2019, Tamar & Jo).

decisions. On the other hand, in the case of collaborators not knowing each other, the designer might have to accept a more comprehensive briefing from the director or even the producer. In this case, it is important for the designer to consider a work offer very carefully. It is important to do some research on the kind of work the director, company or producer tend to do and realistically judge one's own interests, skills and aspirations. The collaborators with whom designers associate themselves play a major role in the kind of work designers produce, how their career develops and what industries they work in. The influence a team has on its members cannot be underestimated. Designers tend to produce different work with different teams. A designer has most control over their output by choosing the projects and people they get involved with very carefully.

Working Alongside a Set Designer

The set design is as crucial in a production as the costume design. One is an extension of the other. Both design aspects need to be rooted in the same concept. They need to operate in the same world that has been constructed by the creative team. That does not mean that both, set and costume, need to have the same approach, but there needs to be a logic to the form both design aspects take. For example, the set design could be an abstract space, whereas the costume design could be in period. Like any approach, this needs to be thought through and make sense conceptually. Both set and costumes need to be balanced carefully and should not compete with each other on stage. The costume designer is well advised to consider the set designer's thoughts and decisions throughout the process and liaise with them on a regular basis.

It is quite common for the director to meet with the set designer first, involving the costume designer at a later stage. The order in which those conversations happen often depends on which of the design aspects, namely the set, costume,

lighting, projection and video, have priority. An element of the design might have priority because it is conceptually more important, or it needs to be tested during rehearsals and, therefore, fabricated earlier than some other elements. An aspect of the design might be prioritized because it takes a long time to fabricate it, or the fabrication process is difficult and needs to allow for mistakes to happen. Whatever the nature of the production is, and the relationship and process of the set and costume designers, they need to take each other into account and to make decisions in relation to the other. For example, if the set design is of a brutalist and heavy nature, and this has been decided before conversations about costume commenced, the costume designer needs to respond to this. They need to take a stance and either emphasize this or create a counterpoint.

Considering the overall appearance of a production is the anchor that the costume designer needs to regularly come back to and test against. At some point, it is a good idea to look at the

Lucretia

The costume designer needs to test their designs against the set design of the production. This can be done in a variety of ways, of which one is to indicate elements of the set in the costume drawing, as demonstrated here by set and costume designer Bettina John for *The Rape of Lucretia* (1946, Benjamin Britten).

Another method to test costume designs against the set design of the production is to print out the costume figurines to scale (1:25) and place them into the model-box, as demonstrated here by set and costume designer Bettina John for *GHBoy* (2020, Paul Harvard).

costume and set design together, using the set designer's model box and scale versions of the character costume drawings, for example. This could be done with the real model-box or digitally in software, such as Photoshop. Another approach could be using elements of the set design, especially colours and patterns, as a background for the costume drawing.

The Venue

The venue has a tremendous impact on how a production feels and how a costume design can, or should, be approached. Every venue holds opportunities but also comes with a different set of challenges. Some stages are narrow but deep, some are wide but shallow, some are simply just small, some feel extremely vast and slightly cold, some invite for a site-responsive approach, some have flexible seating that offers more options, and some are even suitable for a promenade production, where the audience walks with the action. This could mean that the audience comes in close proximity to the performers, giving the audience the chance to examine the costume from up close. Performers might even enter the audience or audience members the stage. There might be

an organized event where audience members are invited to view costumes before a performance and even touch them. This is an opportunity for visually impaired people, for example, to examine the costumes and get a better understanding of the piece.

It gives the designer a great opportunity to create interesting details or to consider interesting design solutions, when audience members are seated close to the stage, allowing the audience to take notice of them. This could open up options to use intricate fabrics and patterns, details that would get lost in a larger theatre space where audience members sit far away from the stage. For larger auditoriums, the designer needs to consider their choices regarding visibility and effect from afar. The designer might need to focus on silhouettes and colour, as these will be the main elements that translate all the way to the back of the auditorium. Equally, a greater distance could give the designer exciting opportunities for their designs.

Site-specific or responsive, as well as outdoor, performances ask for yet another set of considerations regarding the costumes. The atmosphere of a location could influence the design, or the design could be a response to it. Costumes might need to support the visibility of the performers in an environment that is less contained compared to the theatre. This might result in a particular colour palette, for example. In film, this is often the responsible of the production designer, who will work closely with the costume designer to achieve a balance between the environment and the costume.

An outdoor performance might require the costumes to keep performers warm or shield them from the sun. After all, costumes are clothing, and clothing needs to meet functional demands as well as aesthetic ones.

The Cast

The cast is another important consideration for the costume designer. As with the above parameters, the cast too is an element that is mostly out of the control of the costume designer. It is rare for the designer to be involved in the casting, although sometimes their opinion might be appreciated. Conversations with the creative team about the openness to different gender choices or a gender-fluid approach could be initiated by the designer. Decisions like this could greatly impact the design. In most cases, however, the costume designer will have to work with whatever cast choices they are presented with, no matter what their idea of the character might be. In an ideal scenario, the costume designer has knowledge of the cast before commencing the design process. However, this is also not always the case. Ideally, a character is cast in a way all members of the creative team envision them but in reality, that is not always possible. Additionally, cast choices can change at the last minute. That means the costume designer needs to stay flexible throughout the design process with regard to the body shape and appearance of the character. In some cases, a costume needs to be heavily adjusted to a cast member that had been very differently imagined. Not every costume suits everybody. The costume designer needs to respond to this. Furthermore, when finally meeting the cast, their input will also have to be considered. This concerns their particular take on

a character, response to a costume and, potentially, their approach to gender. The performer's ideas about, and approach to, a character might not always be in line with those of the designer or, indeed, the director. These scenarios require diplomacy, flexibility and, most of all, a creative response. That might mean that a compromise needs to be found, or the designer uses their persuasion skills. Taking the performer on the design journey and making them feel part of it, is another approach that could work.

THE CRITICAL COSTUME IN DESIGN PRACTICE

When designing costumes, it is important that the designer reminds themselves of the potential costumes have to be critical. While the function of costumes in the context of performance is, first and foremost, to support the portrayal of characters, the costume can be instrumentalized in many other ways. An audience might have a stereotype or expectation of a particular character or role, which is more often the case than not. A costume can subvert these expectations or stereotypes. It can be a useful tool to overturn audience expectations by presenting a surprising or even provocative version of a well-known character, for example. This can shine a new light on a character or play. A costume can manipulate the audience into making certain judgements on a character in order to then reveal a plot twist. This subversion can be used to various effects, such as helping the audience to identify with a character, to manipulate a change in emotion from the audience toward that character or to make a point about social change, for example. The costume designer might want to make use of this potential when developing a costume concept. Such considerations need to commence early in the process and will have to involve the director and possibly the producer.

Furthermore, it is worth mentioning that the costume has the potential to be the carrier of meaning beyond the portrayal of a character and beyond

Costume design and make by artist and designer Anna Kompaniets, who creates wearable art using sustainable and recycled materials. While creating magical and surreal pieces that take the wearer on a journey and make them part of the story, her pieces are also a constant reminder of the importance of looking after the environment and changing habits toward a more sustainable life. ALLA SANDERS AND ANNA KOMPANIETS

the themes of the play. When envisioned, and sometimes incidentally, costumes can capture the current social backdrop, as many period productions and films exemplify.

The reader might find it interesting to hear that costume exists as a discipline outside the relatively strict boundaries of a stage or film production. The costume can be the starting point for an exploration, which could result in a performance or film. The costume can be a vehicle to explore the body, movement or materials, for example. The costume can invite and dictate how the body moves. A narrative could be created through material and shape. Some designers and scholars use costume as a platform for a scholarly discourse surrounding performance-making, the body and space. A number of costume professionals and scholars debate the various agencies a costume possesses, and some investigate those outside the traditional performance context. Some costume designers consequently exhibit their work in gallery settings or show their work as part of a performance art showcase.

The scope of this book does not allow for a deeper investigation into this subject matter, but the reader, as well as the designer themselves, of course, is encouraged to look beyond the traditional conception of the costume and study the many artists concerning themselves with such work, and the books and publications available.

Costume design by Daphne Karstens for *Session #1, #3, #4* (2019, Daphne Karstens, dancer: Lorraine Smith).

Concept collages by designer and illustrator Jocquillin Shaunté Nayoan for Cecily and Algernon of *The Importance of Being Earnest* (1895, Oscar Wilde), created as part of the UAL Costume Design for Performance course, 2020. It is important to look for inspiration beyond fashion and costume references, and sometimes helpful to look for images of people that come close to how the character is envisioned.

The further reading list at the end of this book can be consulted for more information. It can be helpful for some inter-disciplinary designers to consider alternative terms for their work and practice. Some practitioners, for example, choose to refer to their experimental costume approach as wearable art, costume sculpture or wearable sculpture, while other practitioners deem it important to maintain the term costume. Such nuances could be helpful when applying for funding within the art context or when attempting to show work within a gallery setting. It could encourage the designer to understand their work in a slightly different way and shift the audience's perspective. Using alternative terms to describe experimental costume work could assist when searching for such work online or in books. The various pathways a costume designer can pursue

as a career will be further introduced and examined in Chapter 7.

THE DESIGN CONCEPT

Having gone through the steps described up until this point, it is now that the designer will be in a position to assemble the overall costume design concept and, subsequently, start designing for the individual characters. The main parameters are clear, the research has been done, the world of the piece has been discussed and decided on, the style and form of the piece are clear, and ideas have been explored and tested in the form of collages, sketches, draping or writing. The costume designer has been liaising with the set designer and other relevant creative team members and

Concept collages by designer and illustrator Jocquillin Shaunté Nayoan for Gwendolen and Jack of *The Importance of Being Earnest* (1895, Oscar Wilde).

has got an overall idea of how the design should look and work. It is important to note that this does not imply that the design is complete; it signifies that the designer knows what they want and has a good idea of how to visualize it. From this point onwards the focus needs to be on making decisions and visualizing the designs. It is important to keep the above-introduced parameters in mind during the following process and to be aware of what is expected and what is possible throughout the production process but, particularly, when the actual design is being assembled.

Before zooming in on the individual characters, the overall design concept needs to be clear and outlined, otherwise the designer runs the risk of developing quite different designs for each character that might not come together in a coherent overall design concept. Now is a good time to write out all the information obtained so far and

summarize the design concept in a few words. This will challenge the designer to focus in on the most important information, as well as streamlining it. A vigorous focus on these notes throughout the process of the production will undoubtedly lead to a stronger, more convincing design.

Design Elements

Part of developing the costume design concept is deciding on a colour palette, textures, shapes, silhouettes and, of course, materials, specifically fabric. In order to make decisions on these aspects, referred to in this book as design elements, it is necessary to take the production concept and themes as a starting point and to make those decisions in relation to them. Choices over the design elements could either be in opposition to the themes or could enhance them, and they need to make sense within the world. The designer could respond to the themes playfully, undermine them or exaggerate them. The visuals of a production have a major role to play. A lot of the time, visuals are not in the audience's consciousness and transpire information without clearly stating them. This can help to achieve a certain degree of desired friction or harmony in moments of the play. A designer who understands this fully and has the ability to work this into the design is a great asset to a production. Some details will inevitably change when developing the individual character designs; and some decisions will have to be reconsidered due to new circumstances arising during the making process, from the director's response and, not least, the actor's input.

THE COLOUR PALETTE

At this stage, considering the overall colour palette for all character designs needs to be prioritized, as opposed to focusing in on individual characters. Having said that, it is essential to keep the individual characters in mind. More about design elements for individual characters can be found in

Chapter 4. The choice of colour plays a tremendous role in the communication of ideas. Colour helps to distinguish the characters. Colour can help to draw attention to a character or to let a character disappear into a group of performers or, indeed, the set. Several characters might be organized into one group and colour can support this visually. The various groups need to be considered in relation to each other and not in isolation. Colour can be utilized to a great effect on an ensemble or chorus. During the performance, the colours of the costumes will be in constant dialogue with the set design.

There are many different ways an overall colour palette can be developed and tested. The use of watercolour or other paints is one of the simplest and most effective ways. There could be a rough outline of a background and an implication of the colours of the set to help see the costume colours in context. Another effective way of playing with colour is using magazine cut-outs and arranging them on a bigger piece of paper. The advantage here is that decisions remain flexible until glued down. Of course, colour palettes can be created digitally too and it would not be surprising if, in the

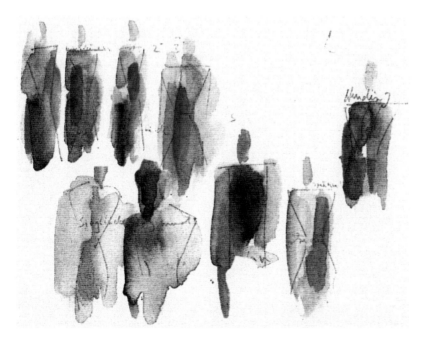

A quick watercolour drawing can assist with the determining of an overall colour palette, as demonstrated here by set and costume designer Bettina John for *The Valkyrie* (1856, opera by Richard Wagner).

future, most designers will have limited their tools to that of the computer. However, there is a lot to say for creating regular opportunities to get away from the screen and engage in the design process in a different way. Doing so will help the designer's creativity. Generally speaking, the designer is advised to use various methods to avoid repeating and referencing themselves.

CONSIDERING SILHOUETTES

The designer will have considered the silhouettes and explored them through collaging or sketching, enabling the designer to make decisions. At this stage, those decisions should concern the silhouettes of the entire cast as a whole or larger group within that, rather than focusing in on individual characters. In a lot of productions, silhouettes need to adhere to conventions of the period the play is set in. In fact, the silhouette is one of the most significant characteristics that help to identify a costume of a particular period, such as the Middle Ages, the Victorian period or the Empire. In other productions, the choice of the silhouette can be approached more freely. In those cases, it is advisable to decide on the focus point of the silhouette, which could be the waist, shoulders or hips, for example. Silhouettes are often named after the shape they resemble, such as the A-line silhouette, hour-glass silhouette, the egg-shaped silhouette or the bell silhouette, to name but a few.

Although not technical terms by any means, they highlight the essence of its shape.

The length of the costumes should also be considered at this point. For example, skirts or trousers might be knee, calf, ankle or even floor length and tops might have long or short sleeves. Long garments, such as long coats, will have a specific impact and jackets taken in at the waist, such as bomber jackets, will have another. While this might be an obvious point, paying attention to such details cannot be underestimated, as their effect is tremendous. In fact, those decisions are not details at all. These considerations too need to be made looking at the cast as a whole.

At some point, if not simultaneously, the silhouettes of the individual characters need to be considered, which this book expands on later in this chapter. It is not unusual to make a difference between the female and male silhouette, and most periods require such a distinction. However, a lot of contemporary productions see the collapse of gender distinction, especially in avant-garde dance, performance and live art but also increasingly in TV, film and modern theatre. Some professionals might argue that approaching gender in a binary way is too narrow and does not reflect society any more. Such conversations will have to be had with the rest of the creative team. It could be a conscious decision to design a uniform silhouette for all performers, regardless of gender.

Rebeca Tejedor Duran exploring colour and shape for Oscar Wilde's *The Importance of Being Earnest* (1985), as part of the UAL Costume Design for Performance course, 2020.

Or the designer might even play around with traditional binary gender silhouettes to create something completely new. Whichever form the designs take, conscious decisions, down to the smallest detail of the design, have to be made.

It Is All About Shapes

Shapes are the elements that a silhouette is composed of. A silhouette can consist of one main shape, or of several shapes. The egg-shaped silhouette, for example, is composed of an oval and the column silhouette is a long rectangle. But a silhouette could be composed of several shapes, such as the A-silhouette, which could be composed of just a large triangle or a smaller rectangle for the top and a triangle for the bottom. Performers on stage are essentially shapes, moving around. A suit could consist of two long rectangles, the jacket and the trousers, resulting in a relatively boxy appearance. This could translate into a casual look, or instead appear clumsy, or even ill-fitting, which depends on the person wearing it and on the fashion conventions of the time. A suit could also be composed of a triangle for the top and a rectangle for the bottom, which might appear a lot more elegant, chic or smart, perhaps trendier. Again, this is dependent on the fashion of the time. For example, in recent years, men's suits emphasize the waist, moving away from the more boxy, casual style of the 1980s and 1990s.

When costumes are drawn realistically, the shapes can get somewhat lost in the detail. In an abstract costume drawing, however, the underlying shapes that a costume is composed of are more prevalent. To begin with, an abstracted costume drawing could help to identify and determine the basic shapes of the costumes. It might be useful here to approach the costume drawing like a painting, starting with the shapes rather than their outlines and then adding the details. This prevents the designer from, literally, getting lost in the detail and losing sight of the main elements of the design.

And Composition

Last, but not least, it is important to touch on composition. Understanding composition is fundamental to a design practice. The underlying balance of a design is achieved by a carefully considered composition, which takes the above introduced elements into account. What is seen on stage could be understood as a carefully composed painting, consisting of elements that appear as shapes, silhouettes and colour. The balancing of these elements makes for harmony or tension, for emphasis on one character and the unison of several others. For example, choosing to costume half of the cast in blue and the other half in yellow will result in a balanced symmetry. The main characters could be dressed in bold colours, whereas

Costume design drawing focusing on shapes, colour combination and composition within a group of dancers by set and costume designer Bettina John for *Alternative Fakes* (2017, choreography Liz Aggiss).

Costume design by costume designer Sophie Ruth Donaldson for *Koottam* (2019, choreography Saju Hari).

the chorus in pastels, which could make for a harmonious picture. In certain situations, this balance could be disturbed by introducing a colour or shape that is alien to the rest of the cast. By doing so, attention can be drawn to one character or situation. The choreography or movement will, of course, play a vital role, without which certain effects cannot be achieved.

As theatre is a durational art form, the designer has to not only consider one image, but a continuous flow of several images in sequence. While this is, for a lot of designers, the appeal, it is also a complex task. This is why storyboarding is such a vital part of the design process and will, therefore, be looked at in more detail in Chapter 4.

The design elements introduced in this section are the fundamental tools of designing. Bringing the above-mentioned design elements of a costume design further into the consciousness is instrumental to a successful costume design. Looking at costume design in this way is no different to painting a picture or choreographing a dance piece. It is about the balance of these elements. The costume designer will have learnt and practised those design elements over years

of studying and working on the job. When mastered, the designer will be more flexible and qualified to work within different contexts and even cross-disciplinarily.

THE CHOICE OF FABRIC

Choosing the right fabric is a complex matter and can be intimidating for a less experienced designer. It is important to know that, in most cases, the designer is not alone and can seek expert advice from more experienced team members. The sheer number of fabrics available, and with ever more coming on to the market, makes it challenging to stay up to date. This overview attempts to lay out the fundamentals; however, it is far from comprehensive. The fabric choice needs to fulfil two main design aspects, that of functionality and that of aesthetics, and both need to be considered to an equal extent, in most scenarios. In order to determine the fabric's suitability, the designer looks at qualities such as drape, weight, texture, colour, material and elasticity. When aiming to achieve a certain look, such as sharp and angular or soft lines, the drape of a fabric and its weight are the most significant qualities. In the case of the

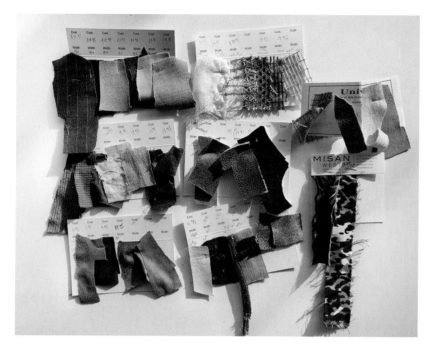

When choosing fabrics for a design, the designer might go fabric sampling in fabric shops or look through catalogues of suppliers. It is important to collect fabric swatches and get a good overall image of the choice, before making final decisions.
SOPHIE RUTH DONALDSON

garment having to sustain a lot of physicality, a robust fabric needs to be chosen, such as a cotton drill or a gabardine, both fabrics typically used in workwear.

It is important to distinguish between costumes that are being bought or sourced and costumes that are being made. When designing, the designer will most likely be aware of this question and be making decisions as they go along. These decisions do not happen in isolation. They are dependent on the budget and resources, such as the number of makers available and how much time they have or whether there is a costume store from which costumes can be obtained free of cost or for a discounted price. When buying costumes, as opposed to manufacturing them, the choice of fabric is less complex. Answers are much more readily available, often dependent on what is offered in the shops and what the garments in questions are typically made from. The designer might want skinny jeans, a classic men's shirt or a trendy summer dress. In these cases, the designer will think much less about the fabric choice and more about the garment as a whole. The choice of fabric becomes incidental, unless

particular features, such as flexibility, are a priority; in this case, a stretch fabric needs to be considered, especially in the context of dance.

Whether fabricated or sourced, in the case of designing for dance, the choice of fabric is vital for obvious reasons, such as flexibility and movement. Garments need to be flexible enough to allow for the performer to move unrestrictedly and the fabric needs to behave aesthetically pleasingly on the body of the moving performer. Of course, what is and what is not aesthetically pleasing is a matter of personal choice and dependent on the concept. Whatever the choices are, the designer needs to take control over the results. When choosing fabrics for dance, the designer is well advised to feel the fabric and test it with respect to its weight, drape and response to light. While these are considerations relevant to all forms of the performing arts, dance costumes are exceptional due to their potentially increased physicality.

Choosing fabric for period costumes, too, needs to involve additional investigation. Many fabrics, as well as colours and patterns available today, were not available in the past. Period costumes have to take knowledge of available fabrics

Fabric is ordinarily stored and consequently displayed and sold on a roll of either 1.40m, 1.20m or 1m. In most shops there is a minimum amount that needs to be purchased. This can vary between 25cm and 1m for independent fabric shops and several meters to a whole roll for wholesale.

and patterns, as well as colours of the time, into account. The older the period, the more limited the fabric selection and colour combination can be, as some colours and fabrics were not yet available or too expensive for characters other than those of royalty and aristocracy. It is worth trying to find vintage fabric originating from the period in question, keeping in mind that they might show signs of ageing, resulting in a slightly different effect to how they were originally intended. That might be advantageous, for example, in cases where costumes need to look worn and faded. Furthermore, when using vintage fabric, the ability to wash and iron them needs to be considered. If the vintage fabric found would not sustain the washing and ironing required or if stretchy material is preferred, it is worth looking for a modern version of the same fabric. All fabric choices, especially those with patterns, need to be considered regarding their effect from a distance, as touched on in the section 'Venue' above.

Fabrics are best chosen when seen in reality, rather than in photographs. This could be achieved by looking through a range of samples sent by fabric suppliers or by visiting places that sell fabric. The first time the designer or their supervisor ventures out to find fabric, they will collect samples, on which basis a selection of fabrics can be made later on. Often, when looking for fabric, it is worth collecting a range of samples from as many suppliers as possible. Making a short video of the fabric's behaviour when moving will help the decision process. It is important to make a note of the shop, cost per metre, width, name of the fabric, how much is left on the roll, if it is low on stock and any other details that can be obtained from the supplier, such as the materials the fabric in question is composed of. Some shops will be very helpful with providing instructions on washing or the necessary amount, but some will be less helpful or will encourage the purchasing of excess fabric. When considering fabrics, in some scenarios it might be important to know whether any of the performers have an allergy to a certain material.

The process of choosing the fabrics for a design will be greatly eased by the designer having a clear idea of their designs and its fabric options, and, if applicable, communicating this effectively to the costume team. It can be difficult to pin down exactly what fabric a garment needs to be made from. If this is the case, an alternative way of approaching the search for fabric is defining what qualities it should possess, for example, its weight, drape, elasticity and colour. Sufficient preparation and good organization are vital when searching for fabric, which often requires visiting many different places in a limited amount of time. It is worth preparing all information needed for this task in a

Design process and fabric selection for the dance piece *I'll See It When I Believe It* (2018, Theo Clinkard) designed by Sophie Ruth Donaldson (in collaboration with choreographer Theo Clinkard).

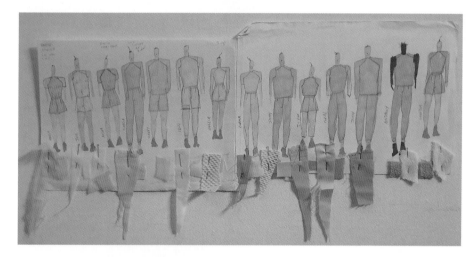

Costume designer and maker Sophie Ruth Donaldson carefully chose fabric and colour for each performer of the dance piece *I'll See It When I Believe It* (designed in collaboration with choreographer Theo Clinkard, 2018, choreography by Theo Clinkard).

Examples of polyester wool and various types of thick cotton. While natural materials are often favoured over synthetic materials, it is worth considering good-quality mixed or fully synthetic fabrics. However, it is important to be aware of the difference in quality that is available on the market and what can or cannot be achieved with it.

clear and easily accessible form, for example, in a transparent sleeve, showing the designs on one page and all other necessary information on the back. When engaged in a large-scale production, the designer might visit various costume professionals and departments within the building or site of a theatre or company to determine the fabric choice. This also requires good preparation, even though the setting is quite different compared to that of fabric sampling in various shops.

A Brief Overview of Fabrics

It is worth looking at the subject of fabric in a little bit more detail at this point, as it plays such a major role in costume design. Fabric is the material most costumes are made of, although other materials, such as leather, felt, fur, hair or various types of plastic, could be used as well. Elements of the costume design beyond the clothes, such as accessories, hats and wigs, will certainly involve many other materials.

NATURAL VERSUS SYNTHETIC

It is fundamental to understand that different types of fabrics are made of different materials, which are either natural or 'manmade', also known as 'synthetic'. Materials are processed into fibres before they can be further processed into fabric. Natural fibres are typically made of silk, cotton, linen and wool. They are either derived from animals or plants. Many fabric innovations have been made since the development of the more traditional fabrics. Beyond polyester and nylon, there was the discovery of viscose, also known as rayon. Viscose is considered to belong to a third category known as 'manmade cellulosic'. While often referred to as 'natural', it needs to be pointed out that fabrics made of this material have undergone heavy processing before they reach their final form. In an attempt to make fabric production and its use more sustainable, many innovations have been developed, such as the use of fruit skin, algae or manmade protein fibre, which all challenge conventions of fabric categorization.

Examples of fine checked wool and various types of linen and cotton.

Synthetic fabrics are solely produced through a chemical process and are predominantly made of plastic and additional chemicals. Over the decades, since the first appearance of such fabrics, many different types and variations have come on the market, particularly those known as 'mixed-fibres', which refer to fabric composed of both natural and synthetic fibres. Synthetic fabrics can pose certain challenges but can also be hugely advantageous. Polyester, acetate, nylon and acrylic, to name but a few, are made from plastic, which is the main reason for most of the issues people report to have with them. They can adapt less well to body temperature, are not as effective in absorbing body moisture and are more prone to odours. However, technology is ever advancing and great improvements on these issues can be observed. A lot of mixed-fibre fabrics are more durable and less prone to creasing. Some mixed wool fabrics perform, in fact, better than the original pure wool form: they can be washed and ironed at higher temperatures than pure wool or silk and good-quality versions can last longer.

Synthetic fabrics might not always look as high-quality, which is often less important in a theatre environment, as the audience might be seated further away from the stage. In the film setting, however, this might be less desirable, as the camera tends to come very close to the actor, which exposes the quality of the fabric and makes it easier for an audience to pick up on the details. High-definition cameras have improved visibility, making it even more important to pay attention to the details. In the film context, period accuracy, too, is more of a concern, when fabric details might give away its origin.

It is also important to understand that fibres can be processed in different ways resulting in the various fabrics available. The two most important methods to know about are weaving and knitting. With these two methods hundreds, if not thousands, of different fabrics can be fabricated ranging from light, to medium and heavyweight qualities, fine to robust, soft to rigid. These different qualities can achieve very different effects. A careful consideration of the demands of the garment is necessary to make the right choice. It can be a challenge to know for certain whether the choice of fabric will be successful, especially if less experienced or dealing with lesser-known fabric. Sometimes the designer has the luxury to make a prototype from the fabric in questions. Depending on how important the choice of fabric is, it might be wise to trial it on the performer and even on stage. An experienced designer and maker will be more likely to tell whether a fabric choice will be successful and, therefore, they might be worth consulting, if in doubt.

The best way to learn more about fabric is to look at those in the immediate environment, such as personal clothes, curtains, soft furnishings, bedding and tablecloths. Most products will have a label stating the various materials of which they are composed. Observing how materials, specifically fabrics, behave, what their drape looks like and how they reflect or absorb light, is a key exercise for a costume designer. This will help to understand fabrics and judge their suitability for a specific context.

SUSTAINABILITY

Fabric production has caused major damage to the environment. While some people condemn the use of synthetic fabric, others argue that it is the sheer amount of fabric being used. So-called sustainable fabrics and materials are being developed, only to turn out not to be that sustainable after all. As a costume professional, it is increasingly important to develop an awareness for a sustainable use of materials and to investigate the sources of fabrics and what the production process entails. Furthermore, it might be worth investigating options to recycle materials, fabric, garments or costumes when working on a project.

FABRIC DYEING

The costume team regularly needs to consider the dyeing of fabrics. This is because the perfect combination of material, quality and colour is often not available. Fabric dyeing is a common process, and most theatres and film production companies have their own dedicated department. There are a few different dyeing techniques and which one

Dyeing fabric can be done in a washing-machine or by hand using a bucket or a more professional set-up such as the example shown in this photograph (by Sophie Ruth Donaldson). Since temperature plays a crucial role in the process, a good control mechanism should be ensured. However, in some cases, it might be possible to approach the dyeing process more casually.

to choose is not least dependent on the material. Some fabrics can be dyed at high temperature, whereas others need to be dyed at lower temperature. The average dyeing temperature is 40°C, which can be done in a washing machine or a bucket with water of the correct temperature; the latter requires regular stirring to avoid staining. Instructions enclosed in the dye packaging need to be followed precisely. Dyeing often involves the adding of salt and sometimes vinegar to ensure the permanence of the colour. It is important to bear in mind that synthetic fabrics are much more difficult to dye and they tend to require much higher temperatures to take the dye. For that reason, only a couple of dye brands claim to be able to achieve it. However, most professionals will report varying degrees of success. On the other hand, synthetic fabrics tend to keep their colour longer and are available in extremely vibrant colours or even in neon.

COMMUNICATING A COSTUME DESIGN

The Costume Drawing

Before expanding a little on the character costume drawing and its purpose, it needs to be said that,

while they are a great and popular way to present a costume design and the best way to explore and show personality, they often require additional information to constitute a complete costume design. The character drawing constitutes only one element of the complete design and is not the only way to achieve it. As opposed to a character drawing, the complete design needs to give information on all aspects, such as the costume's front and back, its colours, fabrics, accessories, costume changes and hair and make-up. This could be in the form of technical drawings of details, for example, such as a hat or glasses, additional garments, such as a jacket and a drawing of relevant underwear, an appliqué or shoes. By the end of this, the design is much more than just a drawing – it is a concept. Furthermore, the complete costume design needs to consider and include all characters or cast members and costume changes to be complete. After having given some more information on the character drawing itself, this section will come back to the overall design and its presentation.

Costume drawings are intended to show what a particular character at a particular moment in the play is supposed to look like. Beyond that, a good costume drawing allows for so much more information to be extracted, such as the character's position in society, what time, country and culture

This design presentation by set and costume designer Bettina John for Fricka and Wotan of *The Valkyrie* (1856, opera by Richard Wagner) includes the costume drawings, information in the form of reference images and a colour palette, which can be done in this way or using fabric samples.

Fricka and Wotan

the character lives in and what kind of life they live. It allows judgement on a character's status and their financial situation, whether they look after themselves and what they care about. The costume drawing needs to clearly visualize what the designer's vision is: first, to the director and, later, to the costume team and actors. Before arriving at the final drawing, the designer will have made innumerable decisions, significant, sometimes difficult ones, as well as those that they are barely aware of. They will have decided the exact style of costume, the colour, length and the exact fit, whether it is slightly dirty, crinkled or in an immaculate state, freshly washed and ironed. The costume might need to be slightly too big or slightly too small. It might be the case that the designer wants a performer to wear trousers that are slightly too tight, to insinuate a certain message. The possibilities are endless, but the context of the play will make it clear. A careful observer would be able to tell a whole story based simply on the costume. A good designer is aware of every single aspect of

the costume and knows how to package this into a drawing. The bigger the discrepancy between the drawing and the designer's vision, the more likely an unsuccessful design becomes. The next section goes into more detail about what exactly a costume drawing is, what a good costume drawing constitutes and why this matters so much. The costume drawing is inevitably intertwined with the design process. While going through the process of drawing the costume for a character, the designer is developing a character and is making crucial design decisions.

The Purpose of Costume Drawings

A costume drawing represents the decision process that a designer has been through together with the director and the rest of the creative team. It communicates the visual world of the play. If successful, the drawing style will give an idea of the overall vision of the production, such as what style and form it will take and what the mood and atmosphere will be. In other words, the drawing can make conceptual statements. The designer's influence on the character development can be substantial. The designer might bring some visual references that spark the director to develop a character in a certain direction. A costume drawing might be the starting point for the director to develop a character and might help the actor to find an approach. Beyond all of the above, the drawing has a very practical function. It is an instruction for the costume team who will make the costume.

A costume drawing gives detailed information on the character and allows judgement on:

- How old a character is.
- What member of society they are.
- Whether they are rich, poor, a member of the working class, an aristocrat or royal.
- Whether they look after themselves.
- What their character traits are, for example, whether they are vain or do not care much about how they look, whether they are fashionable, like to spend money on clothes or pretend to be somebody else.
- What culture and country they come from.
- Possibly, what profession they have.
- Whether the character does manual work and how frequently.
- In relation to each other, costume drawings show the observer whether a character is different from the rest of the characters and how.

A costume drawing allows for conclusions regarding the play itself and could tell the observer:

- What country the action happens in.
- Whether the context is the city or the countryside.
- What period the play is set in, possibly even the exact decade or year.
- What season, temperature and even time of the day it is.

- What the context of the play or scene is. It could be the setting of a factory, an aristocratic house or a garden. It could be set around a festive occasion or a funeral.
- It could give more specific information on contexts such as going to bed or cooking.
- It indicates the period in which the production is set.

A costume drawing contains information for the costume team and enables makers, e.g. the tailor, milliner, wigmaker, shoemaker and buyers, to proceed with their work by giving information on:

- Colour, colour combination and colour palette.
- The kind of fabrics and materials required.
- Dyeing, printing, appliqué or embroidery requirements.
- The fit and cut of the garments.
- Whether they need ironing or whether they have to be dirty, crinkled, new, old looking or worn looking.
- Drawings enable buyers to shop for specific items of clothing, footwear, accessories and haberdasheries.
- Costume drawings need to hold information on hairstyle and headwear.

A set of costume drawings gives information on the characters as an ensemble:

- They show contrast and relationships between characters.
- They show character groupings, mainly through colour and texture.
- They tell the observer something about the characters' class and occupation or their status.
- They show the observer how a company of actors will look as a group of characters for the various acts and scenes.
- They show the costume plot of an actor, i.e. how the costume changes might work over the course of the play or the journey of a costume throughout the piece.

Costume design by set and costume designer Takis for *Die lustigen Weiber von Windsor* (1849, music by Otto Nicolai and text by Salomon Hermann Mosenthal).

The Complete Costume Design

The designer will arrive at a point when the design needs to be made presentable to the creative team and, later on, to the makers. This means that the design needs to be put into a form where it is clear, easily accessible and readable to people with varying degrees of involvement in the design process. This is also a great opportunity for the designer themselves to review the design and to get a good overview of what has been achieved up to this point. Major decisions will have been made and now need committing, and assembling, into a document. This document can contain character drawings, but not necessarily. Indeed, it could also, or instead, contain mood boards, colour palettes, a character overview, fabric samples, pictures of drapes on mannequins

or models, reference images and notes. This can be in the form of a digital file like a pdf, a jpg or, indeed, an online document compiled with platforms, such as Google docs. It could be a hard copy with several extra items glued or stapled on to it, to name but the most common ways. It can consist of one page or several. This will need to be supported with a verbal presentation and continuous communication. Parts of this document become instructions for the makers or buyers.

The costume design and all the decisions made in conjunction with it will remain subject to change or, indeed, not all decisions might even have been made yet. Instead, the individual design will go on a journey and undergo changes, improvement and refinement, which will manifest in various notes accompanying the design, additional sketches,

Male and female Kittens

The Mad Hatter

The Duchess with soft toy

A costume drawing ordinarily goes on a journey after it has been signed off by the creative team to be realized. This process inevitably manifests in the form of notes, marks, additional reference images and fabric swatches stapled on to it. These costume drawings, by set and costume designer Bettina John, for an adaptation of *Alice in Wonderland* (1865, Lewis Carroll) demonstrate this very well.

scribbles and marks from the many people handling it.

It is also common practice for one member of the team to set up a folder online, using platforms such as Dropbox, which the team can access, as well as add information to. It could contain the design but also rehearsal notes, rehearsal footage, reference images and documents of any changes that have been made. The costume designer could create and manage their own costume folder within that and regularly update it. However, care needs to be taken when sharing confidential material, such as photographs of performers, especially while being fitted.

DESIGNING FOR DIFFERENT GENRES AND FORMS

As argued in the Introduction, the costume design process for the various genres and forms is not fundamentally different; however, the following sections will list a few particularities to keep in mind when designing costumes for film, theatre opera and dance.

STAGE VERSUS FILM

The most obvious difference between performance for stage and that for film is that one is live, while the other is recorded, edited, sometimes heavily, and mediated by means of a camera. This inherent difference means that one is unfolding live, while the other is not and can be watched repeatedly at any time. A theatre play will never be the same twice, it cannot stop in the middle of its performance and it can only be watched in a particular place, at a particular time. This results in a few specifics a designer has to consider, for example, in film and television, the importance of continuity and the effects of the camera. Furthermore, technology gives film and television productions more possibilities to create naturalistic and fantastical worlds. Whereas most theatre productions have to resort to a slightly more abstract telling of a story, especially when it involves events impossible to create in front of a live audience without the benefit

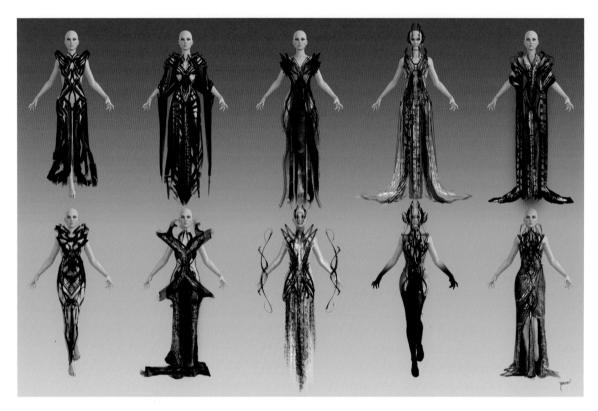

Illustration for costume design options by concept artist Phillip Boutté Jr for Supreme Intelligence of the science fiction film *Captain Marvel* (2019, directed by Anna Boden and Ryan Fleck, costume design by Sanja Milkovic Hays).

of time and editing. This is both the challenge and the beauty of theatre. The distance to the characters, be it the camera or the stage, will have a major effect on the design too.

It will be more useful, for this section, to neglect the many great exceptions, cross-overs and bold experiments where the fundamental differences between the live and recorded arts have collapsed, for example, theatre productions that use live cameras. There is a growing cross-over of film and theatre, resulting in many new particularities posing challenges as well as potential, yet to be discovered.

A designer will find that a higher degree of experimentation with form is possible, if not desired, when designing for stage, particularly for opera, contemporary dance and many fringe and off-Broadway productions. A higher degree of abstraction and stylization is accepted, if not

even expected. However, short film and independent film productions might also leave room for the designer to work in a more experimental way. It often depends on the production and the professionals involved. The various and ever-growing types of technology that can be utilized to create film and TV, such as digital cameras, high-definition ones, as well as lower quality cameras, the iPhone for example, have led to many different forms and styles. Less dependent on the technology used, film splits into feature length films and short films, some of which can be incredibly form challenging and avant-garde.

The use of the camera in film and TV requires the designer to take into account a few particularities. The camera can come very close to the actors, showing a lot of costume detail, which means everything needs to be accurate. A period production, for example, that is set prior to the invention of sewing machines, requires costumes to not show any top stitching. In the theatre, the audience is seated further away, preventing them from seeing these kinds of details. However, that in itself can be a challenge. A particular pattern can disappear, or a texture might not translate far enough. Depending on how far the audience will be seated away from the stage, the colour, texture, shape and pattern need to be intensified. For film, the designer might have to do the opposite and reduce the use of strong colours and patterns. Furthermore, some patterns interfere with the camera; certain fabrics can 'flare' on camera. This usually depends on the pattern and the type of camera. A checked shirt might interfere with the camera lenses and, therefore, needs replacing with a one-coloured shirt. A very vibrant colour or pattern might draw too much attention to the actor when seen in the camera frame. Up until now, highly saturated red tones have caused problems to the software in digital cameras. Furthermore, bright white costumes can be an issue on cameras but also on stage. White costumes on stage can be washed out by the lights and, therefore, need dyeing to a slightly darker shade. Sometimes it is possible to arrange a camera test with the costumes before filming.

Another major difference between the live and the recorded arts is the way productions are prepared and produced. Live art productions go through a period of rehearsals before they open. What follows then is a 'performance run' of exactly that same performance, apart from the variance any action that is unfolding live has inherent. In most film productions there are no rehearsals. A film is produced through a series of shooting days that, in the case of feature film productions, can easily exceed the theatre rehearsal period. The director will repeat a scene, of which most will be recorded, until they believe they have a good version or even several versions. The rest of the making of the film will occur by means of editing the individual scenes. For practical reasons, mainly, the shooting of a film will not be done in chronological order and may jump forwards and backwards in time

repeatedly. This has implications for the costume team. Firstly they need to determine the costumes worn in each scene and then what this means with regard to the shooting sequence. It is important to understand exactly the journey of a character's costume to ensure continuity; otherwise a character might wear a dress in one moment and the next minute a T-shirt and a pair of jeans, without ever having had the chance to change.

One day of shooting can be incredibly expensive, more so than a day of rehearsals for a West-End show, which is why the team has to be well-prepared for the day. The smooth running of a shooting day will be ensured by a team of costume professionals, known as the running wardrobe, specifically the costume standby, also referred to as the daily. They provide and look after the costumes during the shooting. The designer

Costume illustration by concept artist Phillip Boutté Jr for the fantasy film *Maleficent: Mistress of Evil* (2019, directed by Joachim Rónning, costume design by Ellen Mirojnick).

and their team will have prepared several costume options for the scenes shot on the day, just in case a colour or pattern does not work, a garment rips or any other changes of circumstance occur; for example, when the weather changes and the character suddenly needs a raincoat. The costume standby will be available at all times to handle these situations.

Continuity is a major focus in film, as film is not shot in sequence and can undergo heavy editing, as mentioned earlier. It may be that the first half of a scene is filmed weeks apart from the second half, so keeping track of the costume is important. It could also be that the character gets in a fight and gets blood on them. Keeping track of which scenes require the clean costume and which require the bloodied version is vital. The costume standbys monitor that the costumes match any scenes they have previously been used in. They have exact knowledge of whether sleeves were rolled up or not, for example, or which hand the character had their watch on. The costume standby ensures the costume looks good on camera and is in line with the designer's vision. Sometimes after filming has been concluded and after examining the edit it will be decided to re-shoot a scene weeks or months later. It is important that the costume team have a record of what the actors wore and how they wore it in every single moment of the film. Any costume information of this kind needs to be minutely documented. In order to do so, it is important to photograph and document each actor in their costume and to create a bible of what they wore in each scene. It requires a highly organized mind to have an understanding of when the characters wear what and when they change. More information about the various costume roles will be given in Chapter 5 (The Costume Team).

In recent years, it has become much more common to record theatre productions, initially to

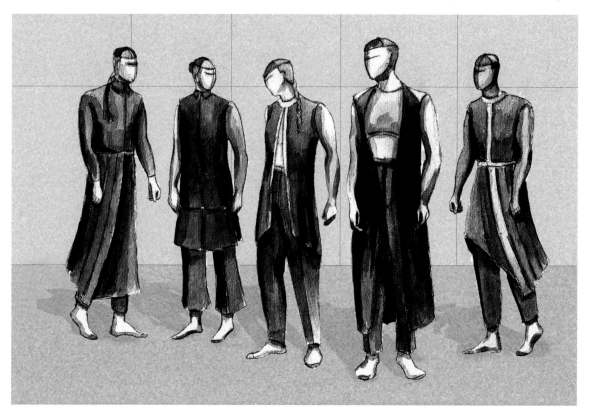

Costume design by Bettina John for the dance piece *Area Squared* (2014, choreography by Tony Adigun).

archive them, then to broadcast them to cinemas to make them available to a broader audience and, more recently, to make it available on demand long after the show went live on stage. It is certainly worth finding out what the producer's future plans are regarding that, to foresee later demands on the costumes. It can be observed that the recording of theatre shows is becoming increasingly complex and professional, to the point where it can be compared to feature film operations. Utilizing several cameras to record a theatre production has become the norm. Sometimes, this might even affect the lighting of a stage production.

Both in film and theatre, often, it is expected that the costume conceals the microphone or battery pack or both. It is worth establishing early on whether there will be microphones. During filming or rehearsals, the placement of them is usually a collaboration between the wardrobe department, sound department and performer. It would only usually be a design consideration if the designer planned to have a very exposed or transparent costume. Obviously, any sign of the microphone breaks the illusion of the film or play, and the magic is lost.

Industries and the technology change fast and the costume designer needs to be able to adapt to new circumstances. The better the fundamental understanding of design principles is, the better the designer will be able to do so.

On Dance Costumes

While conclusions can quickly be made that costumes for disciplines such as dance, physical theatre, acrobatics and circus need to withstand a much more vigorous performance and allow for enough flexibility to move unrestrictedly, there are a few less obvious differences that set designing for dance apart from theatre or opera. Dance is by nature an abstracted form of storytelling. There are varying degrees of abstraction within dance; contemporary dance being the most abstract and classic ballet or physical theatre being on the more narrative end of the spectrum. This abstraction alters the design process slightly, most notably the part of character development. The more abstract a piece, the less realistic a character, hence a different approach to character development needs to be applied. In fact, it is useful, when designing for dance, to think less of characters and more of ideas and concepts represented by bodies moving in space. This shifts the focus more toward abstract thinking and the realm of silhouette, colour, shape, texture and material that expresses most the sentiments of the piece. The designer might want to think about groupings, relationships and images in sequence. Contemporary dance sees a lot of fashion designers getting involved in the designing of costumes. The overlap in the design approach is much greater here than it is anywhere else in the performing arts.

When designing costumes for contemporary dance, the designer needs to study the choreography, the movements, mood and atmosphere and make sense of it. The costumes can then be used to support this. A major task when designing costumes for dance is the organization of bodies, which will then help the audience to make sense of what is unfolding on stage. Designing for dance could be thought of as painting, only with the addition that this painting changes its formation constantly. The reduction to an abstract form, rather than direct storytelling, requires the designer to focus even more rigorously on the fundamental design elements such as composition, shape and colour. One of the tools from Chapter 1 (Understanding Themes and Motifs Through Vocabulary) about finding vocabulary that describes themes in a play, can be of great use when designing dance costumes. Well-chosen and well-organized costumes can help the audience to understand groupings. They can help to unify bodies on stage but equally can be used to make bodies stand out, acting like a focal point in a painting. This means that the designer will focus more on an overall concept, rather than detailed ideas on individual performers. In fact, it is not rare for dance costumes to be conceived as a collection, in which each outfit clearly comes from the same idea and is merely a version of the others. That way a greater unison or indeed separation can be achieved. Dance costumes can still be characterful, but it is more of an idea of a character, as found in circus and mime.

The nature of designing for dance often leads to a greater involvement of the designer in the making process. A lot of designers, designing for dance, have an interest in costume-making or at least aspects of it; in fact, a lot of costume designers generally have. Although a designer does not usually need to manufacture their designs, undoubtedly it is incredibly helpful if there is a basic or even thorough understanding of the making process. In Chapter 5 (The Costume Team), this book will go into much more detail about the different roles and responsibilities within the costume department and when and where there is an overlap. For the design of dance costumes, particularly, a good understanding of pattern-making and fabric is incredibly beneficial. The overall notion that fabric for dance costumes needs to be stretch fabric is looking at the making process from a limited point of view. While stretch materials certainly help, it is the costume's pattern that determines the range of movement possible. For example, surprisingly, the more fitted a garment is the more likely it is to allow for unrestricted movement. Side panels will often be cut on the bias grain to create a small amount of stretch at this key point. Adding gussets, stretch panels or elasticated waistbands can also solve issues of movement. The pattern is inextricably intertwined with the design of the costume, for example, where it has volume and where it is closely fitted to the body. This will have a great impact on the pattern required and, consequently, on the freedom of movement.

Conversations with the dancer can help to determine what is required from the costume. Basic movements will have to be possible across all costumes within a cast, but it might be the case that some performers do not require what others do. This offers opportunity to allow for slightly more restricted costumes for some performers and, therefore, more design options. Some dancers, for example, will need a fitted waist for partner work, while others may require knee pads for floor-work. This may need to be considered in the design by creating a feature of it or covering them up, for example. Often dancers will be upside down, which carries the risk of exposing parts of the body not meant to be seen. In these scenarios, considering what is worn underneath becomes part of the design. Early on in the design process, the designer is well advised to find out how much floor-work there is involved in the choreography. As well as determining this for reasons relating to practicalities of the costume, it is also important to know because a lot of floor-work will draw a lot of attention to the floor. A focus on the floor as a backdrop will have a strong impact on the appearance of the costumes. Finding out what colour a floor is likely to be is, therefore, an essential first step.

A Brief Note on Designing for Opera

Opera productions tend to have a long production period, often one to three years, with several meetings long before the company goes into rehearsals. Designs will often have to be delivered far in advance and often involve hundreds of designs.

EXERCISE

Exercise 1: Creating Colour Palettes

Create a colour palette by choosing a handful of colours from magazine cut-outs. Repeat this with specific themes or a focus in mind, such as spring, summer or autumn, moody, pastel or bold. There are several apps available that allow for the playing of colours and combining them into a palette that can then be saved. After that, try and recreate these palettes using, first, watercolour, then gouache and then acrylic. Observe the different outcomes and take notes.

Exercise 2: Practising Composition

Practising composition can be done by playing around with shapes on a piece of paper, for example. To begin with, cut out a range of different pieces from magazines and arrange them on an A3 piece of paper. Photograph the various results. Revisit them by looking through the photographs and reflect on them. What effects have you created and how. Do you see tension in one and balance in another? Why?

You could practise a different version of this exercise whereby you draw shapes, using chalk, on an A3-size piece of paper. Practise how you can create a balanced arrangement of circles, for example. Then repeat this on a second piece of paper, but this time try to achieve tension. Repeat both versions several times.

The same principle could be applied using a mannequin as a canvas and pinning fabric pieces on to it. The various results should be documented and examined afterwards.

4

ON CHARACTER DEVELOPMENT

Character development is one of the most important tasks in any narrative-driven performance piece, whether this is film, opera or theatre. The designer develops characters mostly in collaboration with the creative team or the director. It is important to address, early on, concerns about stereotyping and casting, including gender questions, so that these can be taken into account when developing the design. First of all a good creative team will attempt to develop an overall concept for the production and an overall costume design concept. After this has been concluded, the costume designer can start developing individual concepts for the characters in response to this. This moment is as crucial for the costume designer as it is for the director. Character costume drawings are often the first manifestation of conversations on character between the designer and the director. Consequently, character drawings have a great influence on the director's vision and, later on, the actor's interpretation of the character.

The designer will most likely have had thoughts on individual characters before this point, particularly when exploring ideas, talking

to the director or when analysing the script at the beginning of a production. The designer will have addressed several questions relevant to the development of the characters, but they will have done this in a general way. Now they can use all of this information to develop their character designs.

A good starting point could be to return to the script and the questions and tools introduced in Chapter 1 and expand on them. For example, a designer might need to design a costume for a female character of a play. Information such as her name, rough age, profession, career trajectory, where she lives, her social status and the relationship to the other characters may be directly obtained from the script. With all this information in mind, further, more complex questions can be asked, such as whether she is happy, loves the people around her, what her relationship to her own body is, whether she cares about her appearance, dresses appropriately or follows the latest fashion. A lot of answers can be found in the script in an indirect way. There might be clues in the text and searching for them can feel like putting together a puzzle. Most likely, however, the designer will have to find some interpretations themselves, possibly consulting the director in some cases. A character might say something about another character that gives possible answers to a question. This female character might have a brother who mentions that she loves to dress up. Living

OPPOSITE: Costume design and make by set and costume designer Bettina John for *Success Cycle* (2017, Belinda Evangelica) (Headpiece and beadwork by Anna Kompaniets)

in the city versus in the countryside will perhaps have an effect on her desire to be on trend too. Also, her cultural background and possibly religious beliefs would influence what she wears. Her profession will have an influence on her way of dressing for practical reasons, as well as expectations certain professions place on the way somebody dresses.

The designer will have to come to the most logical conclusions taking into account the script, concept and the world developed by the creative team and the research they found. Costume choices need to be backed up with research and reverting to stereotypes should be avoided. A person working at the till in a supermarket, for example, might feel no need to dress up when going to work. Their focus might be on practical clothing. On the other hand, this particular character might use any chance they get to dress up, whenever they are outside their work environment. However, it could equally be the case that this character indeed loves to dress up when going to work, despite the need for more practical clothing. Furthermore, the designer needs to think about whether a particular costume should purposefully not suit a character or be ill-fitting to make a point about them. Of course, the cast will also play a role when developing a character; however, as pointed out at various points in the book, the designer might or might not have details on the cast when designing the costumes.

Facial expressions, gesture and stance play a crucial role in the depiction of a character, as demonstrated in this costume design by set and costume designer Bek Palmer for the children's tale *The Elves and the Shoemakers* (1812, Brothers Grimm).

DIFFERENTIATING CHARACTER

Main Characters

The main characters are who the story revolves around, who the story is about and who seem most relevant to the plot and its development. There can be several main characters and sometimes the lines can be indistinct. A new production of a play or a film could also focus on a character that traditionally has not been considered a main character. Clarifying this with the creative team is always an important first step before any character design considerations can commence.

is not about them, nor are they always absolutely crucial to the telling of the story. Equally, a director might decide to shift the focus of the story from a main character to a supporting character and tell the story from a different perspective, from their perspective. This can be achieved by changing the text slightly or simply by the way a director directs a play. Cecily, for example, a character in Oscar Wilde's play *The Importance of Being Earnest*, is, in most productions, not considered a main character, it is Earnest, also known as Jack, also known as John. The director, however, might decide to focus on Cecily, Earnest's ward. By doing so, the creative team might be able to focus on different themes, change the story and its message slightly or even subvert it.

Supporting Characters

The supporting characters are there to help the story come alive or to create tension or a problem but, as opposed to the main characters, the story

Chorus/Ensemble

A chorus or ensemble is mostly understood as one unit, potentially acting as one character. It must be understood as a group rather than individuals.

Madame Butterfly is the main character in the opera of the same name. This needs to be reflected in her costume, as demonstrated in this costume design by set and costume designer Nicky Shaw for *Madame Butterfly* (1904, Giacomo Puccini, libretto Giuseppe Giacosa and Luigi Illica). When comparing these to the other characters of the same production, such as those displayed earlier in this book, this point becomes particularly clear.

Its main purpose tends to be supporting a scene, character or message. However, that does not mean that the ensemble is less important, in fact, rather the contrary. Its ability to support a message can be exploited to a very effective degree, simply because of the number of performers it can consist of. An ensemble can be used to support the main character in one instance but, at a later stage in the play, can be used to support another character or group. It can help set a scene, for example, a street scene, by making up the various people on the street. Designing costumes for an ensemble is, therefore, quite different to designing a costume for a single character. An ensemble offers the designer and, in fact, the director a chance to make a statement, whether subtly or much more overtly. A big group of people can have a great impact on stage, especially in a bigger venue, where audience members might sit far away from the stage. The designer might utilize the chorus by choosing a strong colour code for its members, for example. A chorus consisting of thirty members or more, all dressed in black, red, or black and white, for example, would have a tremendous impact on stage.

Characters in Relation to Each Other

Although an obvious point, it is important to be aware of the different kinds of characters in a play and to take this into account when designing the costumes. In order to do that, the characters and their costumes must be considered in relation to each other. One costume can only stand out in relation to the others or in relation to its environment. For example, if there are five performers in yellow costumes and a sixth one in blue, this one will stand out. The one standing out needs to have a reason to do so, as it will attract attention. If it has no reason to be different, it will mislead the audience into believing there is something special about this character. Of course, there are endless nuances to this simple example.

Since the performing arts are drama and not real life, differences between characters often need to be enhanced and that means the costume might need to be exaggerated in its intention to be different or, indeed, the same. For a play about a city worker, for example, walking down the street surrounded by many other pedestrians, the costume designer might choose to dress the pedestrians in grey costumes and the protagonist in a more colourful, more nuanced costume. The audience can immediately determine who is important in this scene. This character will most likely be one of the main characters, whereas the group of pedestrians will most likely be the ensemble. However, in reality, a crowd of people on the street will not all be dressed in grey; that is the additional drama added by the creative team to tell the story. On a side note, singling out a character may also be achieved through, or in combination with, lighting.

There might be various clues in the story explaining why a protagonist is different to the rest of the characters. It could be their social status, their personality, their body or their behaviour, to mention but a few. These reasons can give the designer incentives for a costume design different to the rest. For example, the protagonist of a particular story might be part of a group of friends that all dress in a similar way, because they are friends. However, the costume designer might need the protagonist to stand out hence giving them a slightly different costume to the rest of the group. Depending on the story, the costume designer can choose to make them appear very different or just subtly different. Most likely, however, there will be a reason in the text why this character is different, which will be intertwined with them being a protagonist. They might be shyer or quirkier or they could be poorer or richer than the rest of their friends. They could be from a working-class background, whereas their friends could be from a middle-class background.

The costume designer has a great pool of possibilities to manipulate the audience and their perception. This is one of the great joys of being a costume designer.

Costume design by set and costume designer Bettina John for *The Valkyrie* (1856, opera by Richard Wagner) showing the protagonists Wotan and his daughter Brünnhilde in an eye-catching red costume and the chorus in the back in more muted colours.

HELPFUL TOOLS

The following sections offer a handful of tools that help to explore characters individually. Some designers use them, some use a version of a couple of them and other designers have developed their own tools. Whatever the approach is, the designer will have to develop design methods to ensure a long-lasting career designing costumes.

Quotes

As mentioned in Chapter 1, paying attention to what characters say about each other is a helpful exercise specifically at this point. This can be done in quite a methodical and thorough way, as suggested in Chapter 1, by putting it into a chart, which additionally helps to visualize the findings. Alternatively, notes can be taken in a less structured way, allowing for further thoughts to be added immediately.

Ask Good Questions

The art of asking the right questions is a desirable skill and crucial in developing a character. The designer could start with asking practical and simple questions, such as what the character is doing, what they are going through and what they need from a costume in order to get through that. For example, do they need a raincoat or a jacket, do they need long sleeves, do they need a formal dress or suit for an interview, for example, or do they need a very warm and cosy jumper? The designer might have a set of questions they always ask at this stage. This could be a way of ensuring that the most important points are raised. The costume design for a character is a document of all the answers that the designer, often together with the director, has found, and the conclusions that they have come to. The magic about a good costume design is that it speaks more than a thousand words. It tells us the story of a person without actually spelling it out. The costume does not literally say, my character is rich, but it gives the onlooker hints, sometimes very obvious ones and sometimes much more subtle ones.

Finding Real People

One of the most useful tools, when still searching for a character, is to look for them in real life. Going to public places, for example, or searching through photographs or paintings of real people on the internet, in books or magazines, can be very insightful. Some designers have built up a character library over the course of their career. Designers who design costumes for story-based performance are storytellers themselves, only that their story is visual. A lot of designers have a genuine interest in people and characters, and enjoy spending time observing people or even starting a conversation. The early career designer is well advised to go out to public places and observe people and their interactions, make notes and sketches.

Figurines

As outlined in Chapter 2 at length, searching for the right figurine can be very helpful. The figurine could undergo many changes over the course of attempting to illustrate the costume. Going through the process of looking for the right one, considering its stance, posture, attitude and body shape, helps to develop the character.

APPLYING DESIGN ELEMENTS TO INDIVIDUAL CHARACTERS

The following sections briefly expand on the earlier-mentioned design elements, by exploring their role in the individual character costume design. An important consideration is to determine which characters need to stand out. This consideration will have been made earlier but needs to be revisited when developing the individual characters and, most importantly, it needs to be manifested in a character costume design. The various design elements introduced earlier will now be the tools to achieve these differences between characters. A character can be created to stand out or fade in with a crowd, for example, through colour, a choice of fabric, texture and silhouettes. The various design elements need to be considered for other reasons too, such as the choice of fabric for practical reasons and silhouettes to reflect a certain age, for example. The following sections will give a few examples on how to utilize the design elements to respond to practical demands on the costume and to develop a character. However, many individual scenarios can arise during the designing of costumes and cannot all be considered here.

Colour

Every character needs to be examined with regard to their individual colour palette, which also needs to work within the overall colour palette. Colour is a powerful tool. It is the most obvious clue for an audience to understand character relations, such as main characters and supporting characters. Colours can support visibility or take away from it. Pastels and shades of grey, as well as earthy colours, tend to fade into the background. Blocks of colours, especially of the primary colours red, yellow and blue and the secondary colours orange, purple and green, will be more effective

Rebeca Tejedor Duran exploring colour and shape for Gwendolen and John of Oscar Wilde's *The Importance of Being Earnest (1895)*, as part of the UAL Costume Design for Performance short course, 2020.

in attracting immediate attention. The designer needs to use this tool to visually guide the audience through the play. In recent years, a lot of research has been conducted to explore how colour can support visibility for visually impaired people, which the costume designer could take into account.

There are some practical considerations to make, such as whether certain pigments were available at the time in which a play is set. Additionally, historically, certain colours were reserved for people of a higher status. In Victorian England, the death of Prince Albert prompted Queen Victoria

to wear predominantly colours of mourning, such as black and purple, which she extended to her people. Designing for the Victorian era, therefore, means a fairly limited and dark colour palette. The following Edwardian era neglected those in favour of lighter colours and pastels in a much greater variety. Every period has a particular colour palette, which the designer needs to consider.

Colours can have symbolic meaning, but the designer needs to be aware of cultural differences in their reception. A wedding dress, for example, is white in most European and North American countries. In other countries, however, it

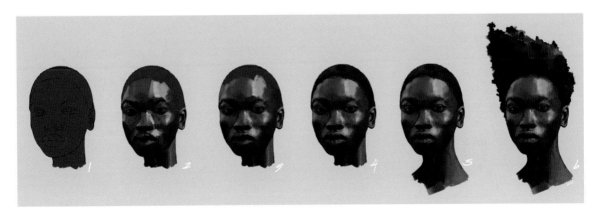

Illustration showing digital painting techniques by concept artist Phillip Boutté Jr, using Photoshop, by firstly building up layers of colour, starting with the darkest value, using a blending brush to smooth the edges and finally adding highlights.

traditionally might have a different colour, such as India and a lot of the African countries. Whether or not a specific colour has a specific symbolism attached to it will mainly depend on the culture, time and context of the play and its specific production. The designer is required to conduct thorough research when wanting to make use of symbolism effectively.

The designer might spend a considerable amount of time finding or mixing the exact colour shade they are imagining for a specific fabric. Using the correct skin tones and hair colour in a drawing should also not be underestimated as a means to determine what a cast member would suit best. Often this can take practice. Blonde is rarely yellow and the tone of the skin on the face can often differ slightly from the rest of the body. The exercises on colour proposed in earlier chapters might assist in improving these skills. A look at the colour wheel to learn more about the mixing of colours is highly recommended. Simple rules, such as adding some green when there is too much red, will be very helpful.

Fabric

The choice of fabric is an important indication for a character's social status, whereby silk and cashmere, for example, look more expensive and could be used for a character with a wealthier background. Victorian aristocracy, for example, predominantly wore silks in black and shades of purple. Some types of cotton or less expensive polyester for younger fashion periods or contemporary designs could indicate clothing of lesser quality. Types of cotton and linen are traditionally used for workwear due to their robust nature. Whether peasants or factory workers, most would have worn less colourful clothing made of these fabrics. However, these general ideas around fabric might not always apply. It is important to consider the exact circumstances of the play and the time it is set in.

The choice of fabric for an individual character has many practical implications; first and foremost, how physical they are. Other questions such as the longevity of a fabric might be important and whether it can be washed and ironed.

Costume design and make by costume designer Sophie Ruth Donaldson for (left) *Starchitects* (2019, Motionhouse) and (right) *Stunners* (2019, Tamar & Jo).

The fabric choice also depends on the silhouette the designer wants to achieve for an individual character.

Composition

The designer needs to consider the individual character design in terms of its hierarchy within itself and not only in relation to other characters. Composition is one of the main tools to use here and to achieve a certain balance within a costume. This might mean that the designer has to make a choice, for example, whether to give the top of a costume a vibrant colour or an exaggerated shape or maybe the bottom instead, consequently focusing on either colour or shape, top or bottom. In some cases, it could make sense to do both – use a vibrant colour and exaggerated forms. The designer could use angular silhouettes to achieve a certain aesthetic and add strong colour to enhance it. Or they might use soft fabric, resulting in a less defined silhouette, subtly supported by pastel colours. The use of colour, pattern, texture, shape and silhouette all need to be considered; for example, whether the silhouette comes in at the waist, whether there is an emphasis on the shoulders or whether to use a patterned scarf or jumper. In a lot of cases, the designer will have to choose which of these elements to prioritize. They might decide for a voluminous top in a vibrant red, but adding a voluminous bottom might disturb the balance of the silhouette and lack dynamic. However, a small change could easily fix this, for example taking in the waist using a belt. Composition is a balancing act of all available design elements introduced in this chapter.

Costume design by Bettina John for *The Rites of Spring* (2016, choreography Ben Duke).

Costume design by Bettina John for *Goddesses* (2011, choreography Arthur Pita).

Consider Lighting

The costume designer is well-advised to work closely with the lighting designer to avoid unintentional effects or, indeed, to achieve certain ones. For example, if the protagonist wears a green costume but the lighting designer wants to use red lighting, the costume may appear brown. Or very shiny fabric can cause unwanted effects under the light, which should be discussed with the lighting designer and/or considered beforehand.

STORYBOARDING (THE JOURNEY OF THE COSTUME)

Theatre is a durational art form in which characters and their costumes undergo changes, which can be small or substantial. These changes reflect what is happening throughout the plot and the characters' journey. The costumes, together with the set and the lighting, reflect how the mood changes over time. They work in combination to tell the story. They can influence how the audience feels. It is vital that the costume designer considers and understands the plot and portrays it through the changes the costumes undergo throughout the play. In order to do so, a good understanding of the plot is necessary.

This will be achieved by reading the script carefully, making notes, possibly using the scene breakdown chart from Chapter 1, and talking to the director and set designer. The journey of each character needs to be discussed to understand the costume needs, including practical changes, such as the need for a jacket, purse or hat. It is important to identify the personal journey each character goes through in a play. Furthermore, additional costume items, such as the jacket, hat or purse, can be used as an opportunity to communicate something further to the audience about the character or mood. Each individual costume item itself, has the potential to tell a story. A jacket, for example, could have safety pins, appliqués and band patches on it, evoking a sense of character. Equally, all accessories could be of the same colour, perhaps making a statement of unity and belonging. However, the designer will have to have an awareness of the audience they are communicating to when making these decisions.

Some character journeys are very easy to identify; for example, the popular coming-of-age story of the nerdy girl developing into a beautiful young woman. While she appears shy in the beginning of the story, with glasses and two ponytails, dressed in an ill-fitting school uniform and old, worn-out shoes, over the course of the story she develops into a beautiful young woman wearing a flattering dress. However, there are many stories where the journey of the character is not as clear. In these cases, a more thorough investigation will be required. Furthermore, the designer might decide not to follow this well-known path and to challenge it. The development of the girl still needs to be clear to the audience though. This might be a challenge and requires a skilled designer and thorough research. This is worth it, as otherwise, the same images and stereotypes for characters would be used over and over again. The designer needs to find a balance between making sure the audience understands the designer's intentions, whilst not over-explaining.

It is worth mentioning that a lot of the characters in a play or film will not go through extensive costume changes. It could be the case that they need an additional jacket, a scarf, a jumper or they only change the way they wear their costume or their hair. It is unrealistic to expect the average person to wear a new outfit every day. Particularly items such as shoes, jackets and scarves will be combined into various new outfits. Often in film or TV, each character will have a 'wardrobe', allowing for a variety of combinations. Designers will often assemble this wardrobe by selecting a colour palette for each character and perhaps a set of shops that the character would most likely shop in.

The journey of a garment seen throughout a play could tell its own story. It could be new and shiny in the beginning but get dirtier throughout the play. This will be achieved by having multiples of the same garment in different conditions. The various stages of its life can be achieved through breaking down and ageing techniques. Even if the ageing of the garment is not visible on stage, it is more often than not unsuitable for a garment to look brand new. In this case, it will have to be washed, creased or dyed. Sometimes simple changes can have a great effect and be absolutely crucial in telling the story. More information can be found on breaking down costumes and who the professionals are responsible for it in Chapter 6.

Costume changes are, of course, dependent on the budget. Sometimes it can be a challenge to

It is important to consider a character's journey throughout the story and reflect this utilizing their costume, as demonstrated here by set and costume designer Bettina John for Rosina of *The Barber of Seville* (1816, Rossini). Rosina's journey, in this production, focuses on her personal growth from a naive girl into a modern woman.

Storyboarding by set and costume designer Nicky Shaw for *Volo Di Notte* (1931, Luigi Dallapiccola).

produce several costume changes for the characters when the budget is relatively low. A solution here could be to use several inexpensive garments and to combine them in different ways to create the illusion of the character changing. That could be a variety of different coloured T-shirts, jumpers, cardigans or the addition of a hat. In this case, it is important to choose individual garments that can be combined easily and are less of a statement piece. It is not unusual, in the context of theatre, to see characters wearing only one or two costumes throughout the whole play. This is widely accepted by the theatre audience, as long as it works within the story. In the context of musicals or film, however, particularly well-funded feature films and large-scale West-End musicals, audiences have grown much more used to seeing the result of bigger budgets. It is important to be realistic about what is achievable within a certain budget. Rather than considering all the restrictions a low budget might put on the design, it is important to get together as a team, early on, and make creative decisions based on what resources are

available. This might lead to interesting and new design solutions and even conceptual innovation. For the adaptation of a classic Victorian novel into film, for example, the director and producer might have initially envisioned it in period costume with a lot of costume changes but then came to realize that this would be too expensive. This might lead to other creative costume design solutions, such as a pared-down version of a period costume or, more radically, setting it in contemporary times. That might seem like a decision too fundamental to depend on budget, in reality, though, this is indeed often the way it happens.

BEYOND CLOTHES: ON ACCESSORIES

Closely linked to tracking the journey of a character is identifying accessories and adding those to the character's wardrobe such as hats, walking sticks, a purse, a backpack, glasses or sunglasses. These additional objects can

As demonstrated in these designs, by set and costume designer Nicky Shaw for *Volo Di Notte* (1931, Luigi Dallapiccola), the designer needs to consider the costume beyond clothes and deliver clear guidance in the form of drawings, notes or reference images to the costume team.

help the character to emerge. They can also help the actor to develop their character. The careful choice of the right accessory in a specific context will greatly add to a better understanding of the character. Accessories can play a minor or, indeed, a major role in a costume design. Whether significant or not, the designer needs to consider, and consequently decide on, all aspects of a character's appearance in their design. Furthermore, it is the designer's responsibility to oversee the making and sourcing of all accessories, shoes and costume props. This often includes hair and make-up. It will be incredibly useful for the designer to build up a strong knowledge of accessories, such as the different types of hats and shoes. The more profound and specific a designer's knowledge is on accessories and how to use them and, furthermore, on the different types of jackets, coats, trousers, etc. available, the easier it will be to communicate with the creative team and, later

on, the costume team. This kind of knowledge is not acquired within a short period of studying or training; instead, it takes years of experience and an interest and the passion to continue learning about it. The designer will acquire more specific knowledge with each project that requires a specific set of accessories of a specific period. The 1940s and 1950s, for example, saw an incredible range of hats for men; this would require the designer to understand the many types of hats, their names and their use. Furthermore, the designer is well advised to research how to wear a specific accessory needed in their production, for example, how to tie a tie. While it can, and, indeed, should be, an enjoyable task to research and study this, it will also be valuable knowledge going forward and is worth investing time in. Generally, whenever time allows, the designer is well advised to learn more about their trade, about costumes, fabrics, clothes, materials and even new ways of designing costumes.

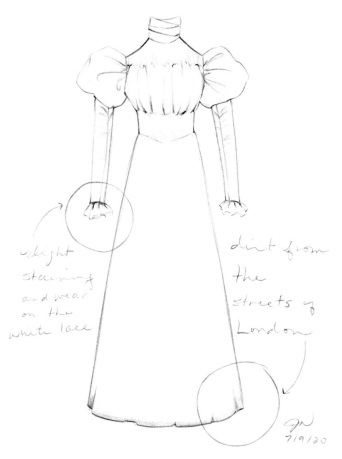

light
staining
and wear
on the
white lace

dirt from
the
streets of
London

7/9/20

Drawing by designer and illustrator Jocquillin Shaunté Nayoan of a costume showing small signs of wear and tear.

rehearsal process with the actors, the idea for a hat, for example, is developed. In most productions, whilst rehearsals are taking place, the designer, although attending some rehearsals, will also be busy sourcing and liaising with the makers or workroom. Typically, the stage manager will sit in on the rehearsals and make notes. These will then be summarized in a document known as rehearsal notes, and sent to the whole team. It is vital to read these on a daily basis and to respond to any requests and changes. Additionally, the designer is well advised to regularly speak to the creative team and professionals in the rehearsal room about any changes, in case they have not been passed on via the rehearsal notes or need clarification. Depending on the production and how much contact the designer has with the director, changes may not always be sufficiently relayed to the designer.

When discussing accessories, the costume designer might encounter overlaps with the props department. This will matter during the costume realization process and in budget discussions. It is also important to clarify responsibility over items regarding its care during the performance run. Often the wardrobe staff will look after the 'costume' items and the stage management will look after the 'props'. Whether an item is a costume or a prop is often resolved by determining whether the item is worn, which then defines it as a costume item. This could also have an impact on flame-proofing. Costumes tend to not get flame-proofed, whereas props do. Often, the distinction between props and costume can be made regarding the concept. Whether realized by the costume or prop team, the costume designer might want to stay in charge of the appearance of the item and provide a design for it.

Accessories might be requested in rehearsals for an actor to begin using as part of their own process. Problems can arise later on if accessories have not been sufficiently rehearsed with. For example, adding a walking stick at the last minute might prove to be quite a big change in how an actor will walk. Furthermore, an actor may become attached to a particular pair of glasses and find it difficult to change to something quite different later on. The closer the rehearsal accessory that the costume team provides can be to the one used for the actual performances, the better.

Sometimes there will be no mention of an accessory in the script or in the early discussions with the director. However, throughout the

Costume roles within film and television

ASSISTANT COSTUME DESIGNER

ASSOCIATE DESIGNER

BUYER/SHOPPER — **ASSISTANT BUYER**

COSTUME DESIGNER — **COSTUME SUPERVISOR** — **WORKROOM MANAGERS**

- COSTUME SUPERVISOR ASSISTANTS
- COSTUME COORDINATOR

COSTUMIER

HAIR&MAKE UP
- HAIR AND WIGS
- MAKE-UP
- PROSTHETICS

Costume makers
- Cutters
- Tailors
- Dressmakers
- Men's
- Ladies'
- Period
- Stitchers
- Fitters
- Assistants

Specialist makers
- Corsetry
- Hosiery
- Millinery
- Embroidery
- Stretch
- Knitters
- Beaders
- Electronics

Wardrobe (Crowd)
- Wardrobe supervisor
- Cutters
- Tailors
- Dressmakers
- Men's
- Ladies'
- Period
- Stitchers
- Fitters
- Alterations
- Assistants

Running Wardrobe
- Wardrobe Supervisor
- Lead costume standby
- Costume standbys
- Costume assistants
- Maintenance
- Laundry
- Repairs

Specialist textiles
- Textile Artists
- Agers
- Dyers
- Surface artists/ Breakdown artists
- Art finishers
- Assistants

Costume props
- Masks
- Armoury
- Jewellery
- Accessories

Footwear
- Shoe maker
- Shoe repair
- Cobblers

Bettina John

EXERCISES

Exercise 1: Silhouettes and Shapes

Isolate the shapes and silhouette of an existing costume design of your choice by tracing it, for example. You could also just study it and note down your observations. Analyse the effect this silhouette has on the body and the story it tells. Repeat this with several designs or reference images, such as fashion plates. Use references from different periods to learn more about their specific silhouettes and their effects.

Exercise 2: Wear and Tear

Choose a garment or a complete costume of a character. Draw it in a simplified, two-dimensional way, like a technical drawing. Circle areas that need ageing and breaking down and think about how this could be achieved. More information on the breaking down of costumes can be found toward the end of Chapter 6. Repeat this for a top, trousers, a skirt, a dress, an overall and so on. Create a backstory or professional context, such as a farmer, a carpenter, a metal worker, a clerk, a bike messenger, etc. for each garment or complete costume.

5
THE ROLE OF THE
COSTUME DESIGNER

While the previous chapters cover the design process itself, this chapter goes into more detail about the role of the costume designer, their team and the reality of working as a costume professional in the performing arts industry. The costume designer's responsibility goes far beyond the designing of the costumes itself. After the designs have been finalized with the director, they need to be presented to the creative team, the cast and the costume team. Often this involves several presentations. The designer needs to get used to presenting their work and ideas, as this is a vital part of their role. The design presentation signifies the end of the first phase – the design process – and the beginning of the second – the costume production process – which will be covered in Chapter 6. During this phase, a collaborative approach is vital and effective communication absolutely crucial. Before handing the designs over to the costume team to be realized, the costume designer and creative team need to make sure that they agree on all aspects of the design, or at least the essential ones. It is advisable to be clear in the communication of the costume design from the beginning of this process. However, it is important to always keep in mind that circumstances can change. A positive attitude toward the design and its implementation can really make a difference in how the costume team responds, especially toward more challenging and risky ideas.

OPPOSITE: This diagram gives a rough overview of the many costume roles that exist within film, without claiming to be comprehensive. Every theatre and film production, television show and opera house will have their own unique personnel and role titles, not to mention the differences that exist between locations.

THE ROLE OF THE COSTUME DESIGNER AFTER DESIGNS ARE COMPLETED

After completing the costume design, the more practical work begins. From this point onwards, situations can arise that nobody could have foreseen, and things can go wrong. This period can be quite a rollercoaster. When the designer hands over the design to the costume team, the designer automatically will have to give up some control. At the same time, it is the designer's responsibility to safeguard the design and make sure that it is being realized in the best possible way, that necessary changes happen in line with the design concept and compromises will not weaken the overall appearance of the design. Being a designer, especially in this phase, requires dedication, precision and perseverance. The designer does not only need to have a strong understanding of the concept, but also be determined. It will be necessary to keep an eye on all aspects of the costume realization process, pretty much at all times. This is a challenging task for various reasons. The designer needs to understand the restrictions set by budget and resources, time, location and skills, and work with them. This requires diplomacy, resourcefulness and imagination. There is no point in trying to push for an aspect of the design when it is simply not possible. In some situations, this might mean having to cut a costume or find an affordable alternative, whilst not losing the overall design aesthetic.

It needs to be understood that the designer cannot take part in every aspect of the costume production. They are required to be present at various other ongoing activities, such as rehearsals and meetings with members of the creative team. Furthermore, most designers will work on several productions at the same time, making their schedule even more difficult to navigate. The designer's availability needs to be clearly communicated to the team to allow for the smooth-running of the production and rehearsal process. Over the years, designers will build relationships with professionals that they continue to work with, which can simplify some of these challenges. It is vital that designers know how to navigate the various environments they work in and how to operate effectively within them. It requires a lot of social abilities to do this. Essentially, being a designer is as creative a role as it is a managing role, which must be understood when deciding for this career path. Effective communication and being responsive to questions raised by the team is the key that will get a designer through any difficulties and obstacles along the way to opening night.

THE MANY DIFFERENT REALITIES OF WORKING AS A COSTUME DESIGNER

It needs to be understood that the reality of working as a costume designer varies greatly depending on the stage of their career, their skills and preferences. Furthermore, it depends on whether the designer works in theatre, dance, opera, film or television, internationally or regionally. The scale of the production, for example, whether they work in fringe theatre, with not-for-profit companies or a touring company, will have an impact on the day-to-day tasks of a designer. Last but not least, the reality of a designer will depend on their financial situation; for example, whether they earn a reasonable living with their design work or need support, whether they get this support and from whom, and whether they need to take on part-time work alongside building a career as a designer. Questions around family and relatives they might have to care for will impact a designer's

reality and influence choices. Access to education and support, work and networking opportunities and industry contacts will also have a tremendous impact on how a designer's career unfolds.

The framework of a production has a great impact on the actual responsibilities a costume designer is expected to fulfil and chooses to take on. Due to budget restrictions, for example, the designer might be required to manufacture or source the costumes themselves. Especially in the beginning of a designer's career, they are often expected to not only design, but also make, source, buy, dye and even help dressing, ironing and keeping the show up and running. The next chapters will expand on the questions or issues arising from this in much more detail. However, it could be the case that the designer likes to take on more roles beyond the design and to get involved in the manufacture or sourcing of costumes. Some designers have a background in fashion design, styling, pattern-cutting, embroidery, costume interpretation or other specialist-making backgrounds and are passionate about these aspects of costume, as well as the design itself. Instead of deciding on either design or making, it is absolutely possible to do both, but it does often require a slightly more vigilant career navigation and search to find that exact niche where all of the designer's skills can be applied.

The reality of the work as a costume designer greatly depends on whether they are in full-time employment or a freelancer, and what kind of company they work with or for. Some designers decide to start their own company or costume studio, sometimes also referred to as 'atelier', and employ costume professionals themselves. However, in theatre, most designers are freelancers. In film, and most certainly in television, this is not necessarily the norm. Especially long-running television series will employ designers, for a certain period at least. Large television organizations will allow early career professionals to grow within their company and, if they have the interest, eventually become a costume designer. Working within a company versus being a freelancer is an entirely different experience and daily reality. It is important

Costume design and make by Anna Kompaniets for *The Alternative Miss World Competition 2018* (1972, Andrew Logan). Artist and designer Anna Kompaniets uses costume as a platform to express her thoughts on moving toward a more environmentally friendly society. Her intricate work relies on meticulous recycling of everyday materials, such as bottle lids, plastic bags, tights and bottle corks and consumer waste with deadstock, end of line and vintage Swarovski crystals. ANNA KOMPANIETS

not to forget that it is always a choice. It is useful to keep in mind that somebody who sets out to become a costume designer can carve out a career that suits them and their personality. Some professionals thrive in the structure of a full-time job, whereas others enjoy the buzz that accompanies the reality of working on several projects at once and constantly meeting new people. It might also be the case that a designer sets out for a career they think they want, only to realize that certain aspects of this career path do not work for them at all. At this point, it is worth searching for other contexts in which the costume designer can operate in a more agreeable way. The designer can try various roles and environments throughout their career and then edit them down to the job that suits their needs and skills the most.

Designer-Makers

Designers who also make the costumes are often called designer-makers. Especially in the context of dance, music and fashion, it makes a lot of sense to have a comprehensive understanding of both aspects and to take on the task of making

costumes or at least partly making them. Some costume designers will have a more elaborate studio set-up that enables them to make costumes and to employ full-time and/or part-time makers or freelancers, on a project-by-project basis, to help make the costumes. In some contexts, such as dance, the manufacture of the costume is closely linked to the design. In such a scenario, it can be a lot easier to be more involved and proactive in the making process. A good understanding of pattern-cutting is a great benefit and, in some contexts, even mandatory. As a lot of designers have a great interest in both the designing and making of costume it is not rare to find those who are equally passionate and knowledgeable about design, as well as pattern-cutting and clothing construction. The lines between these disciplines or roles can be indistinct. It is important never to forget, when working as a designer, that all aspects of costume, all the different roles, require creativity, resourcefulness and skills. Some people decide to combine certain additional aspects of costume into their role, whereas others prefer to only design, make or only do embroidery, for example, and leave the other costume aspects to other professionals.

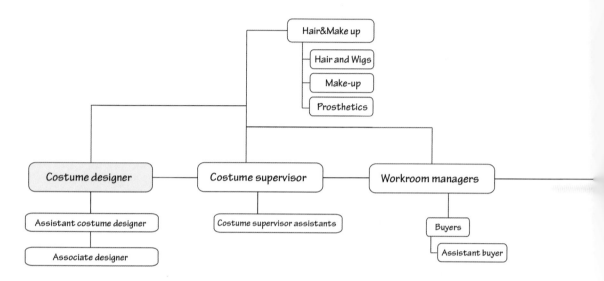

This diagram gives a rough overview of the many costume roles that exist within theatre, opera and dance, without claiming to be comprehensive. These diagrams are meant to give the aspiring costume designer a deeper understanding of the costume professionals they will be working and interacting with. Furthermore, they are meant to give the aspiring costume professional a chance to understand just how many roles exist in this field.

THE COSTUME TEAM

There are a multitude of costume roles within the industry and the designer will work with many of them at some stage in the process of realizing the costumes. Most of the costume roles will have a part in the costume realization process, such as the making or buying. Other costume roles are responsible for the running of live productions or will be on stand-by during the shooting of a film or television programme. The number of people involved in a production, and the roles that exist, vary greatly from production to production. It depends on the budget, first and foremost, the industry, which country the production takes place in and the company or theatre itself. On most productions, the designer will need some support at some point, and costume professionals need to be hired, either by another team member or by the designers themselves. Depending on the size of the production, the designer might need support with a range of tasks, such as fabric sampling, costume sourcing and minor making or

alteration tasks; these could be given to a costume assistant or a supervisor may take on some of these responsibilities. In reality, however, on smaller scale productions, the designer will not have that much support and will have to be incredibly resourceful to compensate for the missing support. In some cases, the designer might need to consider hiring any additional support themselves and potentially carrying the costs. On larger scale productions, however, the designer will work with a team of costume professionals that make and source costumes, and organize and conduct fittings.

Costume-Makers

For many productions, especially larger scale ones, the costumes will be manufactured, rather than bought or hired, and the supervisor, or indeed the designer themselves, needs to look into hiring costume-makers, specialist costume-makers and artists. Amongst them there is a great variety of

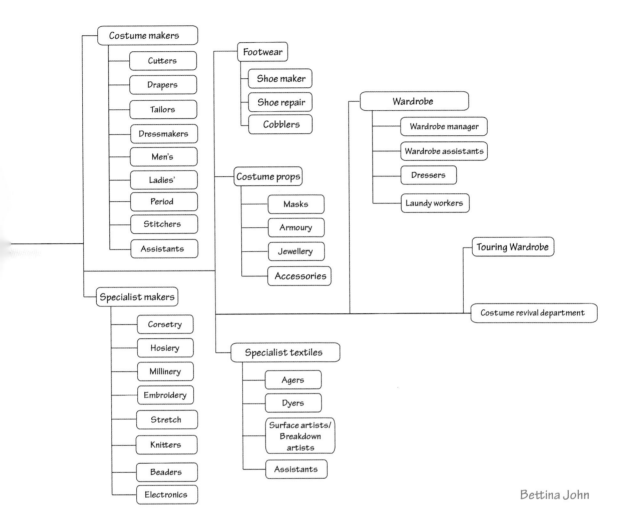

Bettina John

costume specialization, ranging from men's and ladies tailoring to corsetry, millinery and embroidery, and costume prop-making such as armoury and masks. These specialists are vital but not always easy to find. It is worth consulting other designers and professionals for recommendations. The making of costumes could also be outsourced to a making studio that is specialized in the required skill. There are studios that have specific expertise in period costumes, for example, corset-making, the making of ballet costumes, working with stretch fabrics or the making of costume props. These studios often employ several full-time or part-time and freelance professionals. It might be worth asking for recommendations from these studios when searching for a professional.

The Costume Supervisor

A mid- to large-scale production, certainly an opera or a larger-scale musical, will have a costume supervisor, who will be the designer's closest ally. In opera and theatre, a designer will be supported by a supervisor rather than an assistant costume designer, but these roles can greatly overlap. A designer might take on an assistant costume designer or might work with an associate. While this is ordinarily the case in film, in theatre, this is currently rather rare. The supervisor plays a crucial role in delivering the costumes and having a good relationship with them will be extremely beneficial to the designer. They are the first person the designer will consult after the designs are signed

Artist and designer Anna Kompaniets uses a variety of classic techniques in a highly unconventional way, such as crocheting with plastic bags, shoelaces and tights, which allowed her to create new work while recycling materials. This photograph shows costumes for *Quedenraha* (2013, Anna Kompaniets and Lenka Horakova), a performance art piece that took inspiration from the history of the Queen's House building in Greenwich, London. JASON WEN

off by the creative team, and often even before that. Conversations with the supervisor include the budget and what can be achieved with it and the timeline. The designer will discuss with the costume supervisor what needs to be made, what will be bought and what will be hired. As the supervisor is in charge of the budget, they will need to be extremely organized and able to have difficult discussions with the designer regarding compromises based on budget restraints. The designer and the supervisor will talk about from where costume items can be sourced and when this needs to take place. They might also discuss whose expertise is needed. Last, but not least, they will talk about how a costume could be manufactured and what fabrics could be used.

These conversations will often be more general in nature, rather than detailed questions about how a costume could be made. The designer might discuss these at a later stage with the respective maker. A lot of the time, it is the supervisor who organizes the fittings and helps to conduct them, but again, this can vary greatly. A supervisor will look into finding makers and assistants who will source, buy and alter costumes. This often includes the transportation of costumes from a shop to the theatre or fitting location, for example. Depending on the size of the production, the supervisor will also support the making

process and help alter and fit costumes. The role can be full-time, working within a company, theatre or opera house or it can be a freelance role. As a freelancer, a supervisor might build strong relationships with a couple or a handful of designers, with whom they will continue to work, making the supervisor an even more vital part of the team. The supervisor will develop an understanding of the design process over time and be able to step in for the designer, if and when needed, act on their behalf and protect the integrity of the design. Occasionally, in contexts such as large-scale opera and film productions, the costume supervisor will have assistants themselves.

The costume supervisor for film has similar responsibilities but might not work as closely with the designer. The costume designer on a film will be supported by the assistant costume designer, introduced later in this chapter.

Costume Workrooms

A large opera house or a feature film production, for example, will have numerous in-house costume professionals that specialize in a great variety of making. These professionals work as part of a workroom dedicated to a specific aspect of costume-making, such as tailoring, millinery, jewellery,

This is an example of a well-equipped, medium-sized costume workroom, where everything has its place, while offering a friendly and personal atmosphere to the full-time, part-time and freelance staff. (Costume workroom of *The Place* in London, photographed by costume designer and maker Frances Morris.)

footwear, corsetry and hosiery, and textile and surface treatment such as the dyeing and ageing of fabrics. There are workrooms responsible for hair, wigs and make-up and the making of costume props such as masks and armoury. Ordinarily, every workroom has a manager who ensures its smooth running. A costume department tends to have an internal fabric store with a good stock of regularly used fabrics and a buyer or team of buyers who purchase new stock for each production. A lot of these costume roles differ depending on the context and industry, location, size of the production, available budget and the needs of the design itself. All of these costume roles can be found outside the boundaries of an opera house, theatre or production company, and many professionals work as freelancers.

Head of Costume

Opera houses, theatres and some production companies will have a head of costume, who oversees the costume department and ensures its smooth running. The head of costume in an opera house or theatre very rarely gets involved in individual productions and very rarely designs. They are responsible for budgets and the hiring

of permanent costume professionals, for example. To reduce the running costs of an institution, company or organization, the teams are kept to a minimum size and additional costume professionals are hired, if and when needed. Instead of hiring more costume professionals, often work gets outsourced, if necessary. This can be a specialist costume-making studio, instead of individual makers.

Within the film industry, the head of design can be the costume designer.

Costume Assistant and Assistant Costume Designer

Depending on the industry and context, the costume roles and their job titles can vary slightly, but in essence the design and realization process is pretty similar, certainly for a designer. Some of the names of the costume roles can be confusing, especially for people who have had no work experience in the respective industry. The costume assistant, for example, might be worth expanding on, as it seems the most natural role to apply for after graduation or when beginning a career in costume. There is a fundamental difference to point out, which is the one between the costume assistant role and that of the assistant costume designer.

Having a system to store costumes, fabrics, trimming and haberdasheries is vital for the smooth running of a busy costume department. (Costume store of *The Place* in London, photographed by costume designer and maker Frances Morris.)

Depending on the context and size of the production, the costume assistant may not have any interactions with the costume designer and will mostly help with a range of making tasks and alterations in the workrooms or assist during fittings, for example. Often there is another role in between the designer and the costume assistant; for example, the department or shop managers, the costume supervisor or the assistant costume designer. The costume assistant role comprises mostly of making, repair and alteration tasks. It can lead to other costume roles within a workroom, such as a specialist-making role, a pattern-cutter or a senior technician, depending on training and interests. It might also be possible to move into a supervisor role and, with a bit of effort, become a designer. However, in most contexts, such as an opera house or a theatre, it might be a challenge to develop organically into the costume designer role. More about the different pathways for a costume designer can be found in Chapter 7.

The assistant costume designer is a role more common within the context of film and TV, although it can sometimes be found within theatre too. However, in theatre, it is the costume supervisor, mostly, who provides support to the designer. Both these roles work closely with the costume designer and have prospects to be offered designer roles at some stage in their career. The assistant costume designer's work comprises of similar tasks to those for which the designer is responsible, such as conducting research, attending fittings, sampling fabric and safeguarding the design throughout the making process and the shooting. The role of the associate designer greatly overlaps with this of the assistant costume designer but might differ in responsibilities, which can be reflected in a better fee and more prevalent crediting.

Wardrobe Department

Generally, in theatre and opera, the designer will not be in close contact with the wardrobe department. It is the costume supervisor and assistants' responsibility to liaise with the wardrobe team. These costume professionals are responsible for the smooth running of a live performance. The size of the wardrobe team and the roles within it can vary greatly and depend on the industry, venue and production. A production with a lot of costume changes, especially a period production, will need a bigger team, especially professionals known as dressers. They give support to the actors during costume changes and make sure the costumes are well prepared. The team is responsible for small repairs and, in some cases, for the washing and ironing of the costumes. Sometimes this work can be outsourced, depending on the location and theatre. The briefing of the wardrobe team usually happens during the technical rehearsals when they will see the costumes for the first time. Whilst the designer's role will be in the auditorium, watching the costumes on stage, their costume supervisor will be both taking notes from the designer, front of stage, and communicating them back to the wardrobe department.

In Film and Television

WARDROBE

It is worth pointing out that the term wardrobe is slightly more complex in the film industry and comprises of different roles to that in theatre. Work in the costume department is divided between the making wardrobe, which is responsible for the buying and making of the costumes during pre-production, especially for the crowd costumes, and the running wardrobe, which takes care of the organization, maintenance and continuity of costumes during filming. Wardrobe could also refer to the entirety of the costume department, especially when working with professionals originating from the United States. Job responsibilities for costume professionals vary from production to production, depending on the scope of the film or series, and the requirements of the costume designer. As a result, the boundaries between job roles are indistinct, particularly in the case of costume assistants, costume supervisors and wardrobe supervisors.

WARDROBE DEPARTMENT

Film and television productions can have a costume supervisor and a wardrobe supervisor, when in some cases they could refer to the same role. However, on larger productions, the wardrobe supervisor will be the head of the wardrobe team, who is specifically responsible for the manufacturing of costumes for the crowd scenes. This team comprises of its own dedicated cutters, drapers, stitchers, specialist-makers, agers, dyers and finishers. Some cutters will bring their own team on board.

RUNNING WARDROBE – COSTUME STANDBY AND COSTUME ASSISTANTS

During a film shoot, costume standbys and costume assistants ensure that costumes are available when required and maintained in the meanwhile. They are part of a team often referred to as the running wardrobe, mentioned earlier. They assist performers with dressing and the laying out of the costumes. They oversee costume continuity and, in some cases, maintain and service costumes when not in use. After the shoot they ensure that costumes are safely stored, packed and returned to the relevant sources, or sold. Some productions might employ assistants for this work. Sometimes, actors will make specific requests for their standby. As the standby's work involves close and often personal contact with the actor, this role requires excellent social skills and a good attitude. Depending on the scale of the production, the costume designer might or might not be in close contact with the standby. In many cases, however, the costume designer will see the standby in the morning of the shooting day, relaying any updates regarding the costumes used for that day or simply to make sure everything is in order.

COSTUME ILLUSTRATOR

In the film and television industry, it has become more of a reality to have a costume illustrator in the team, who helps with the costume drawing. This can extend to visualizing how an actor would look like wearing a specific costume design. Illustrators are sometimes also referred to as concept artists, depending on the context of their work. Hiring a costume illustrator is rather uncommon in the theatre industry. While the number of costumes and changes can be pretty substantial in an opera production too, a film could easily double and triple that, which makes an illustrator a welcome help.

6

THE COSTUME PRODUCTION PROCESS

The following sections go through the costume production process for theatre, opera and dance, from planning to costume-making and sourcing through to rehearsals. While many similarities regarding the costume-making and sourcing exist between theatre, film and TV, their schedules, planning and time-frames are very different. A section toward the end of this chapter (Form, Genre and Industry-Specific Information) will address this in brief, while some similarities, worth mentioning, are pointed out at the various relevant points. The rest of this chapter is dedicated to a more detailed introduction to costume-making and its various steps.

PLANNING

After the designs have been signed off by the key members of the creative team, such as the director and the producer, the designer will start the realization process. Planning this period realistically, both regarding the available time and budget, will be a crucial step. If there is a supervisor, they will take on a considerable amount of the workload, allowing the designer to focus on safeguarding the design. Independently of whether the designer has access to a supervisor or an assistant or will work alone, before starting this process the following parameters need to be determined:

- The budget available for each character (an even split).
- Changes to the budget distribution (which individual costume might need more budget to be realized and which costumes can be created with less budget).
- The garments that need making, buying, sourcing and/or hiring.
- The places to hire, buy and source garments.
- Any less expensive options or free resources (e.g. costume stores).
- The type of makers needed and who this could be.
- Any other specialists required, such as dyers, agers, milliners, etc.
- The types of fabrics and the exact colours.
- The places where to find these fabrics.
- Dates and deadlines, such as fittings, line-up and dress rehearsals.
- Any other concerns or potential complications.

After these questions have been addressed, the costume realization can be planned and a schedule drawn up. A document called the 'production schedule' should be consulted very carefully at this point. The production schedule is a document created by a production manager, for example, not a member of the costume team or the designer. All team members will have to observe this schedule. The production schedule, also sometimes referred to as the rehearsal schedule, exists outside the costume schedule and considers mainly rehearsal times and the availability of the rehearsal space, actors, singers, musicians and other key roles.

item	price	shop	details if needed	
Lewis				
Lay				
Navy Jacket	55.00	Asos		
Navy trousers	-		using his own trousers	
Off white shirt	5.50	primark		
Belt	-		own	
Shoes black	-		own	
George				
Skilling				
Blue Jacket	51.00	asos	asos, still to sort	needs returning
Blue trousers	20.00	asos		
Light blue shirt fit	4.50		primark/charity	might try and return this
Light blue shirt large	17.00	Tk max		
blue tie	3.50		charity	
Robe	-		own	
Sport Jacket	-		own	
Padding	-		Bettina contributed this	
Glasses	-		own	
Black shoes	-		own	
black funeral coat	-		own	
pocket square	9.00		amazon ordered	
Matilde / Georgina				
Roe				
Blue dress x2	46.00	asos	asos	
Stiletto matilde	2.00	Sue Ryder		might have found one
heels Georgina	25.00	asos	asos	
Leather Jacket	-		from cast	
helmet	-		from cast	
black overcoat	-		own	
large hat	2.75		noemie's	
sunglasses	2.00			
Congresswoman				
stripped blouse	4.50	primark	primark/charity	georgina to bring own
blue/black blazer	40.00		charity/primark	
blue/black trousers	-	primark	charity/primark	
Analyst				
blouse	-		same as above	
blue/black trousers	-		same as above	
The board	-			
sunglasses	1.00		primark	
blind stick	-		props	
Woman				
blouse	-		own ?	
Denim skirt	9.00	Sue Ryder	charity	
Leather Jacket	-		same as above	
Boots	-		her own, still needs trying	
fish net tights	3.00		amazon ordered	
...*				
Gage				
Arthur Andersen				
Bluesuit Jacket	19.50		charity	
Black trousers	-			
Grey shirt	7.00	Sue Ryder		
Business anchor+trader				
Grey shirt	-		same as above	
Black trousers	-		same as above	
tie purple	4.00			
red bow tie	2.50	Sue Ryder		
Court officer				
beige shirt	17.95		amazon	
badges	5.00			
Raptor				
Grey stripped polo	-		same as above	
Black jacket	-		same as above	
Black trousers	-		same as above	
Mask	2.50			
Asos delivery	5.95			
Spent	**838.70**		-	
Budget	1,000.00			
BALANCE before Returns	**161.30**			

* in order to reduce the size of this budget, parts have been omitted

While budgets are the responsibility of the supervisor or head of costume, on smaller productions it can easily be left to the designer. Most budgets are calculated using Excel, independently of whether they are large-scale or small-scale, as demonstrated here using the budget of a 2019 low-budget production of the theatre play *Enron* (2009, Lucy Prebble). It is useful, in some cases, to share the budget chart on a digital platform in order for the costume team, such as assistants, to add to it and keep track.

This document may be constantly being updated. The designer and costume team are well-advised to refer to it regularly. All costumes are expected to be ready to be worn by the actors or performers for the dress rehearsal, which is one of the last rehearsals before the opening. Therefore, all planning needs to be made in relation to this date; however, individual costumes might be required at an earlier stage.

Planning this period is a complex task, as every member of the costume team will have to consider slightly different circumstances. The designer will, most likely, be working on other projects and will have to take the meetings and deadlines of those projects into account when committing to fittings, for example. A lot of the theatre and film workforce are freelancers, which means everybody is working on other projects, requiring them to carefully plan their time and availability. It is always a good idea to be aware of travel time. The designer needs to gauge when attendance and availability is crucial and when their absence will be least disruptive or even noticed. In an ideal world, of course, the designer should be continuously available to the director and costume team, but as this is never really the case, it depends on the designer to navigate this reality sensibly and professionally. For example, in moments when presence cannot be promised by the designer, but is necessary, the designer could arrange for an assistant to act on their behalf, or give more responsibility to the supervisor. Being clear upfront regarding availability and other professionals getting involved is vital and can help greatly when projects become more stressful toward the end of the production process and rehearsals.

Measurements

An important task in the realization process of a costume design, and before the making of the costume can commence, is to obtain the cast's measurements. Measurements can be obtained in various ways and at different times. They could be provided by the performer themselves, which is the least reliable option, although sometimes the only one. In some cases, rough measurements could be helpful to the designer and/or their costume team at an earlier stage of the process. When designing the costumes or finalizing them, it is useful to have the performer's measurements and their headshot, preferably a full-body photograph to understand their proportions. The best option is for the costume team to take the measurements themselves, that way not only ensuring their accuracy, but also their comprehensiveness. It is also the most certain way to avoid any confusion. Ordinarily, the supervisor or an assistant take the measurements. While this is not commonly the responsibility of the designer, on small-scale productions, as a designer-maker or when at an earlier career stage, the designer might need to take them.

Measurements can be taken in various different ways, but it is important to follow one method at a time and to be precise when doing so. It needs to be made clear whether measurements are in centimetres or inches. They should be organized into a table for ease of reading and to avoid confusion. The most common method is to start determining the waistline and marking it by fastening a band around it. A lot of the measurements will be taken from that line or relate to it. When designs exist already, measurements can be taken in relation to them, which might allow for some measurements to be ignored; this will save precious time. However, when the designer is not sure yet, it is best to take all measurements, including the head and neck circumference. As a general rule, the more fitted a costume is supposed to be, the more measurements are necessary to make it, including those of the ankle, calf, thigh and arm circumferences.

SOURCING COSTUMES

When working for a theatre, company or production house, it is possible that they have access to a free

English National Opera
Costume Department.

or affordable costume store. This will vary in size and quality, depending on the theatre. A costume store can not only be extremely cost-effective, but it can also help the designer to find the right direction with the realization of their designs. Turning a drawing into a three-dimensional garment can be a challenge. Some designers see the costume drawing as a starting point, knowing that the realized version could be different. Other designers expect the realized costume to be exactly like the drawing. Buying a costume from a charity shop or a specialist vintage shop, or even getting it made, will offer a lot less flexibility with respect to trying it out and certainly altering it.

Theatres often have free or affordable access to a costume store, while a lot of film and television companies work with costume-hire businesses, such as London-based 'Angels'. A list of other costumiers can be found in the Appendix. A film production company might have built a relationship with a theatrical costumier or a number of charity shops, offering several advantages, such as more flexibility and discounted rates. A staff member, for example, working at the costumier, might be able to seek out items in the stock room and reserve them for the designer, their assistant or a buyer, ahead of them coming. While costumiers, especially the larger ones, are very popular amongst film production companies, theatre production companies use them too, especially those that produce larger shows. The variety of services offered by costumiers is great, ranging from the hiring, making and storing of costumes, to consultancy and maintenance. Hiring costumes, instead of buying or making them, is not only useful for the reasons laid out above, but also more sustainable. Any single costume item that is being re-used, reduces the pollution that otherwise would have been caused by the manufacturing of this garment. Sustainability is a growing concern in the industry and designers need to start paying attention to it.

Clearly, sourcing costumes or hiring will not always be an option. Often, especially when the costume design is contemporary, or after the 1980s, it will be more advantageous to buy costumes from charity, second-hand or vintage shops. Nothing is more convincing than an original garment, genuinely used and worn out, over the years, in exactly the right way. Original blue jeans from the 1980s are most convincing when found in a local charity shop. Original noughties, low-cut bell-bottom trousers, are easiest to come by in a slightly dated second-hand shop. When searching for a vintage or charity shop to visit, it is good practice to consider which area the character would frequent. Most second-hand shops reflect the people living in the area they are located in; however, styles can date back a few years, sometimes even decades. Sourcing costumes from second-hand shops is another more sustainable option than making a new garment for the same reason mentioned above and should, therefore, be the preferred option.

When on a budget, or looking for much less trendy garments, it is best to go further afield and not shop in the most well-known vintage shops or in the city centre. Not only will those shops be overpriced, but they will also focus on the latest fashion. This might not always be appropriate for the character. Instead, an oversized, slightly stained, slightly worn out, knitted old jumper, could well be more appropriate. Finding costumes in second-hand shops is not the easiest of tasks. It often requires endless searching and sifting through rails of clothes, not to mention the weight of the many clothes that accumulate over a day of sourcing. The process can be made more difficult by the necessity to shop for multiples of garments. This could either be necessary because several performers wear identical costumes or because the nature of the piece requires there to be a replacement garment in case it becomes damaged, for example. Other reasons for the need of a replacement garment could be a very long performance run where the wear and tear of some of the costumes is expected. Equally, it could be the case that a costume needs to be available in two different versions: a clean and a dirtied-down one. It may be a challenge to find two or three of the same garments in second-hand shops; this could be solved by purchasing one and using this as a prototype to get two replicas made.

It is often not that straightforward who takes on the task of shopping; it depends on the budget and the designer. There might be a costume buyer or supervisor, who can both be expected to take on these tasks. However, the designer could still decide to join in, just because there is a true interest or an absolute attention to detail. Certainly, when starting out, sourcing will be expected from the designer. A simple Google search for charity shops is a great start, when unsure where to look for shops and how to find them. There tends to be an abundance of them, not only in bigger cities, but also smaller towns. In fact, quite often shops in smaller towns can be surprisingly well stocked and affordable and worth the trip. Fairs, car boot sales, jumble sales and markets are also great places to find affordable clothing, both ordinary clothing and special ones, such as vintage and period items. These places are also great when looking for vintage fabric, lace or buttons. Theatres and opera houses, as well as costume-hire businesses, regularly organize sales to keep their stores to a manageable size or to raise money.

MANUFACTURING COSTUMES

In many cases, costume designs will be realized by manufacturing the costumes or partly manufacturing them, often simply referred to as costume-making. It mainly depends on two factors: the costume budget and whether these garments could be sourced instead. However, other factors can play a role, such as the designer's preference, resources, time and location. In some countries it might be cheaper to make, rather than buy or even order the costumes online. A costume design that has been realized by manufacturing all costumes, rather than sourcing them from various places, may appear more consistent, which may or may not be what the design requires and the designer wants. However, considerations around an environmentally friendly approach need to be considered, in any case.

There is an incredibly wide range of costume-makers available, as well as designers that make or specialize in one aspect of making. Some designers consider the making as part of their design

These images show various stages of the design and making process of costume designer and maker Frances Morris for the costume department of *The Place* in London. When constructing a garment, a sewing machine, as well as a machine known as the 'overlooker', will ordinarily be used. The latter prevents the fabric from fraying. It is also common in the handling of stretch materials.

process. Designers working in this way might not focus on a complete costume design drawing and instead only use it as starting point and an idea of what the realized costume could look like. Such a designer might want to explore the design further through the making process. During the making process, they might further explore qualities such as texture, materiality and shape, unlike other designers, who might have concluded this conceptually, maybe in a drawing.

A good supervisor will have a great understanding of the various making skills and an abundance of contacts to draw from when recruiting a team. When left to the designer alone, it might be a challenge to find good makers. A good maker can add so much more to the costume design, when invited by the designer. It can be incredibly helpful to listen to the costume team's and supervisor's comments and advice in meetings and during fittings. However, most makers will either only give advice when asked or very cautiously; this might be out of respect to the designer. Listening carefully and encouraging the maker to share their thoughts can be very helpful to the designer. A lot of designers will have built up relationships with certain costume team members over the years,

whether freelance or employed, which can make this process a lot easier.

Making is much more expensive than most people would guess. The fashion industry is partly to blame for this, as clothing is available at such a low cost, which does not at all reflect the hours of labour and amount of resources that go into making a garment. As it stands now, when employing a maker in a Western European country or North American country, the cost will seem extortionate compared to a garment available in a high street shop. However, breaking the cost down into the hours spent making the garment and the cost for its material, it becomes clear just how little profit most makers actually make. This explains why answering the question as to whether to make or source the costumes depends on the available budget.

Costumes for performance have to be robust to last through a few, if not many, performances, which can be very demanding. As opposed to garments available in shops, the finish of a costume might not always have to be perfect, but it has to withstand a lot more strain, a lot of sweat and potentially many washes. In a lot of cases, the costumes will stay with the company or production

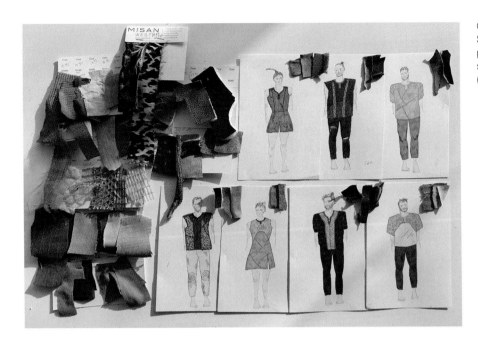

Costume designer Sophie Ruth Donaldson's process of choosing and sampling fabric for *Henge* (2020, Motionhouse).

house. In other cases, they will be sold to start a new life somewhere else. Ordinarily, they will not remain with the designer; however, the designs tend to be the intellectual property of the designer.

Many different people will wear a costume and, therefore, it needs to be adaptable to different body shapes. One important point to raise is to make sure that a costume can be re-used and altered. Unlike the garments offered on the high-street, costume items will have generous seam allowances and an accessable structure to allow for changes. Due to the sheer amount of knowledge that goes into making costumes, this book will not go into much more detail with the making of costumes.

Sourcing Fabrics

When decisions are made to manufacture the costumes rather than to source them, the next step will be to sample and eventually decide on fabric and other materials, if needed; this is a crucial moment – the choice of fabric can make or break the design. A lot of designers and makers love this moment; it can be creative and enjoyable, not least as it marks the transition from concept to realization, and from two-dimensional ideas to three-dimensional creations that can be touched and experienced. Any costume designer will get excited by the sight of rolls of fabric and its various textures and colours. Fabric is to a costume designer what paint is to a painter and clay to a potter. Nevertheless some designers work in a way where there is little to no involvement in the costume-making process; instead, the approach to designing costumes is solely conceptual and two-dimensional. There are literally as many processes as there are designers. However, it can easily happen to temporarily 'forget' about the realization of the costume design when designing and drawing weeks on end without ever entering a maker's workroom or a fabric shop. It is for this reason that a designer is well advised to regularly make an effort to visit fabric shops, museums, exhibitions, charity shops and markets throughout the design process. It is great to have access to millions of images through the internet, but nothing replaces the sensations had when touching fabric or holding a certain kind of material.

Costume-making process by costume designer and maker Sophie Ruth Donaldson for *Rubby Sucky Forge* (2020, Eve Stainton). Before sewing two pattern pieces together, it is advisable to pin them. There are a variety of different pinning techniques. Sometimes, it might be advantageous to check a pinned garment on the mannequin before sewing it together.

The sampling and buying of fabric will mostly be the responsibility of a costume supervisor and costume assistant, if these roles have been filled; otherwise, it goes without saying that this responsibility falls to the designer. More often than not, the designer does get involved, whether there is a team or not. The designer might not follow every step the team takes in order to gather all the materials needed but, when sampling, the designer is very well advised to join in. If this is not possible, and it often is not, the designer needs to make sure that they are kept informed on the findings and choices. The designer should have the final decision regarding the fabric choices. This process can be complex: there will be a lot of going backward and forward, trialling fabrics and putting together a prototype, then sending pictures to the designer or inviting them along to the workroom to look at the results in person. This is also a good moment to look at new fabric sampled on shopping trips from which the designer was absent.

Larger theatres and production companies will not solely rely on local shops and markets to get fabric; instead they will work with fabric suppliers, possibly wholesale suppliers, with whom they often have had long relationships. When considering fabrics and suppliers from whom to order,

the head of costume or the supervisor will show the designer available fabrics in catalogues that contain real fabric swatches. When working on smaller productions, the costume designer might have this option available to them, but the choice will be substantially reduced, as suppliers often require a minimum order. Ordering fabrics online, from eBay sellers, for example, is certainly an option, but always comes with a great risk due to the limitations of a photograph and the lack of touch and real-life sensation. Before ordering fabric online, it might be a good idea to visit local fabric shops and determine exact colour, texture and material, as well as exact descriptions and names of fabrics, in order to do a precise online search, as well as to communicate unambiguously with the seller. To reduce the risk, it would be preferable to order a sample, but this is not always an option. To add to the complication, often fabrics with the same name will have a different weight or amount of stretch. It cannot be assumed that because one Lycra sample behaves one way, that Lycra from another supplier will be the same. If possible, it is advisable to use colour charts, such as Pantone, when liaising about colour. Furthermore, it is important to be aware of delivery times and possible delays.

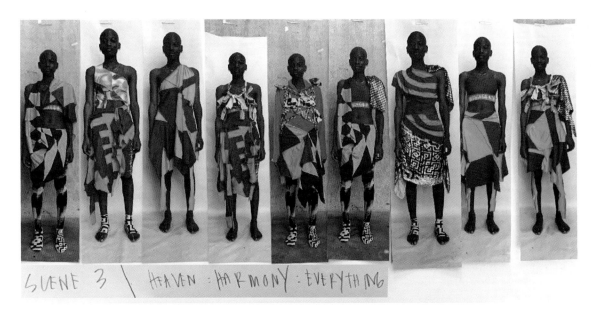

SCENE 3 / HEAVEN : HARMONY : EVERYTHING

Costume design process of multi-disciplinary designer Louise Gray for Wayne McGregor's adaptation (2019) of Christoph Gluck's *Orpheus and Eurydice* (1762) (model Aminat D. Seriki).

It happens regularly that the designer or supervisor finds the perfect fabric in terms of colour, pattern, shine or print but it has the wrong qualities; for example, it is too transparent or too lightweight. A possible solution can always be discussed with the costume team and could result in the backing of the fabric with a more substantial material, for example, or adding a layer underneath a transparent fabric, for example, to become opaque. It is possible to use non-stretch fabric when a stretch fabric is actually necessary by adding stretch panels – which will mostly be hidden by the 'performer's arm' – in the sides of the garment. This allows for more flexibility in the sides while the rest of the garment can be made of a non-stretch fabric. Additionally, this could become a decorative element, and add more texture. This demonstrates how crucial the sewing pattern of a garment is; such techniques are particularly common in costume-making for dance. It is helpful to keep in mind that bespoke fabrics can be manufactured; for example, a particular weave or knit that results in texture or pattern. Furthermore, fabric printing suppliers are easily accessible, and prints can simply be uploaded online to be printed on fabric in

a relatively quick turnaround. The designer is well-advised to get a sample before potentially committing to metres of fabric.

It is important to keep in mind, when sourcing fabric, that there is always an opportunity to do this in a more sustainable way; for example, looking for second-hand fabric before buying new fabric or re-using fabric from old costumes. The types of fabric and their sources could also be examined regarding their sustainability, although nothing is as effective as simply recycling fabric.

FITTINGS

To allow for the timely completion of the costumes, it is important to leave enough time between the fittings and when the costumes are needed.

It goes without saying just how crucial fittings are in the process of realizing costume designs. There can be a great gap between the designer's vision for their costume designs and how they actually look on a body, specifically a body that the designer did not anticipate. Fittings need to be scheduled in a way that they allow for enough time to make changes to the costume. More often than not, there will be changes, which can be substantial. If the designer is aware of the casting for the production they are working on, the performer's body shape and size can be taken into account. This might put some limitations on to the design or open up another avenue; either way, designing without that knowledge can result in some complications later on. This does not mean that the designer has no control over their designs, in the case of the cast not being known during the design stage. The designer can very well anticipate certain scenarios and plan for it. For example, the designer could create a few versions of the same design, possibly for a tall or a less tall actor, or a female, male or gender-neutral version, and in this way, anticipate a variety of cast choices. Fittings are crucial because they show a real-life version of the costume design, which is, more often than not, different to the drawing. Instead of getting disheartened by possible discrepancies, the designer needs to see this as a chance to make amendments and to improve the design.

It depends on the production schedule when the fittings can and should happen, as well as the availability of the actors and the designer, and when the costumes are ready. It is advisable to plan for two costume fittings for the performers playing the main characters and those that have several changes and accessories. Equally, any other costumes that have a foreseeable potential complication should be fitted at least twice.

The designer should always try to attend fittings, as this is the only chance to see the costume in real life and make changes. If this is not possible, the designer can ask a team member they trust to conduct them, such as the supervisor or an assistant, and study any photographs taken during fittings afterwards. Alternatively, the designer might be able to attend through video-conference. Allowing directors or choreographers insight into the costume production process, such as allowing them into fittings or sharing photographs of them, should be considered carefully; this can easily lead to unnecessary complications.

Conducting fittings successfully requires experience. Furthermore, the designer will not always,

and more importantly, does not need to know all the solutions to a problem arising during a fitting. They need to know their designs very well and safeguard these through the process, while experienced team members can give support on everything else. However, the designer needs to be able to judge whether team members have the required experience, ensuring that the designs are in safe hands. A basic understanding of how to manipulate the fit of a garment will be beneficial and, possibly, even required in some circumstances. It will become apparent, over the years of working in costume, that fittings, alterations and maintenance techniques can vary greatly, depending on the costume professional's training and experience. What matters is effectiveness and efficiency, as time is always of the essence. It might be worth stressing here that costumes for stage have to be robust, and repairs and alterations strong enough to last.

The designer should always try to see all costumes together before it is too late to make changes. It is important to see all costumes, their colours, finishes and textures, at one glance not only to judge how successfully the designs are realized, but also to see whether the design itself has any flaws that could still be fixed. When performers start wearing their costumes in rehearsals, it is often too late to make substantial changes. However, some effective changes will still be possible at that stage and the designer needs to be particularly alert during this period.

How to Conduct a Fitting

When conducting fittings, it is vital that the designer also discusses hair, make-up and accessories, such as hats, scarves or glasses. That might mean that the designer has to request them to ensure their availability for the fitting. Furthermore, there is a styling element to the costume that must not be underestimated. For example, questions whether sleeves or trousers need to be rolled up, a jacket open or closed or scarf draped around the neck. These details need to be agreed on and subsequently communicated effectively, to ensure the costume is worn in the way intended by the designer.

During fittings, the cast member will ideally be wearing appropriate underwear. If they need padding or shapewear this should be fitted first. Then the performer will try each of their costumes on and the supervisor, cutter or assistant will use safety pins to take in any excess fabric. Waisted garments will need to be positioned in the correct place; for example, 1950s' trousers will sit high on the waist, while 1990s' trousers may sit lower on the hips. The length of the sleeves and hems will be pinned to the ideal length. Details such as the collar width, pocket positioning or neckline can be judged and corresponding notes taken.

To determine whether a dancer or physical performer has the full range of movement, they need to be asked to move in their costume, ideally trial a range of their most extreme sequences. Safety pins may have to be re-positioned several times during this process. To add to the complexity, in some cases more than one performer will be wearing the same costume. Any adjustments will then need to be documented for each performer wearing that costume and then prepared in a way that it fits all of them. Each costume should be photographed, ideally front, back and sides. In some cases, for a dance piece, for example, it can be useful to take a small film of the costume moving. Usually there will be a mirror for the performer to see themselves in the costume.

More commonly practised in dance and devised theatre, the designer might be part of the research and development phase of a new piece, allowing them to test out their costume ideas with the performers then and there. This gives them a huge advantage when designing the costumes later on. It is a great way to see if something is not going to work very early on, to respond to it and to develop unusual solutions.

FITTING ETIQUETTE

The performer needs to be given the chance to get changed in privacy. The professional conducting the fitting should ask before touching the actor or costume and before taking a photograph. It is helpful to put the actor or performer at ease, giving them a positive and reassuring reaction and listening to their worries or questions. It might be helpful for the designer to keep in mind that a costume fitting can feel uncomfortable to a performer.

The designer is well advised to carry a toolkit with them. In some situations, and they will certainly arise in a smaller scale context, the designer might be required to get practical themselves. In some cases, for example, when time is of the essence, it might be easier for the designer to simply have some scissors available or a safety pin to attend to a problem. In scenarios where the designer is also the maker or is partly involved in the making, it will certainly be necessary to carry a toolkit.

Costume emergency toolkit. From left to right: unpicker, small scissors, fabric scissors, thread in a range of common colours and thicknesses, transparent thread, various needles, measurement-tape, a variety of emergency buttons, safety pins, tailor's chalk, sew-on press buttons of various sizes, hook and bar fastenings, pin-needles, laces or other types of thick thread or ribbon, elastic band, buckles or other types of fastening options. This kit should ideally be prepared for every production.

The picture shows 'piano and stage' rehearsals for a large-scale opera production.

REHEARSALS

The rehearsal period is a crucial time for the designer. It allows them to see their work on stage, often for the first time, with lighting and set. It is the best opportunity for the designer to examine and potentially tweak the overall visual image of the production. Depending on the length of this time, the designer may be able to make some small changes to their design. Attending rehearsals regularly is an important responsibility of the designer. It helps the production immensely if the designer keeps the director or choreographer and the rest of the team informed about their whereabouts and when they can be expected to attend rehearsals. It is worth discussing what the director's expectations are regarding the designer's rehearsal attendance, not least to assess the feasibility of taking on a job.

While for some directors the ideal scenario is having the designer on their side at all times during rehearsals, others work much more autonomously. It also depends on the nature of the piece itself.

Different productions have different requirements. A devised piece, for example, will require the designer to be in the rehearsal room much more frequently, as the work develops out of the interactions of the various collaborators in the room. Some productions require rehearsal costumes, long skirts, for example, or other costumes that require practising in them. There might be a restriction a costume places on a performer's ability to move freely, which needs to be discovered early enough. Sometimes, surprisingly so, performers, as well as directors, enjoy what a costume adds to the piece, so they will attempt to incorporate it. This process should be a collaboration between the performer, director and designer.

For a costume designer, rehearsals split into two different phases – both are equally important. During the first phase, the costumes are still being created and the designer is spending a substantial amount of time in the workrooms, shopping, conducting fittings and liaising with the various departments and team members. That means they are not able to spend as much time in the rehearsal room. The second phase of rehearsals are toward the end of the production, where the costume designer can see all aspects of a production come together and judge the overall image. These are called technical rehearsals. An enormous amount of information can be obtained from attending them. When watching rehearsals, the designer will gain more information on the requirements of the costumes. Furthermore, they can examine whether the costumes support the piece and its concept in the way it was initially conceived. The start of the making of the costumes will, most likely, coincide with the start of rehearsals. The designer or their team can immediately pass on any rehearsal notes to the costume team. At this stage there should be enough time to respond to these; however, while minor design inadequacies can still be addressed, there will not be enough time to re-design the costumes altogether. The disconnect that exists in most productions between the designing phase and the rehearsals can be a challenge and requires a bit of experience, as well as trust within the team.

The rehearsal period can last for anything between ten days and eight weeks, sometimes even longer. Rehearsals require complex scheduling and, therefore, good communication, which is why, especially on larger productions, there will be a role assigned to this task. Ideally, this person, who tends to either be the stage manager, assistant stage manager or assistant director, will put together a document after every day of rehearsals containing notes from the day and send it off to the team, amongst them the costume designer, supervisor or assistant. This allows the designer to take care of other responsibilities, such as visiting the workrooms, fabric sampling or meetings, whilst still being able to participate in the progress made in the rehearsal room.

Technical Rehearsals

In the live performing arts, the last days or week before opening night are called technical rehearsals. They mark the moment when every element of the production, such as acting, set and costume, lighting, music, sound and video, are installed and fine-tuned by the respective teams. The performers will run through the show, while the lighting and sound team make adjustments. This will be the first time the director and everybody else are able to truly judge what they have worked toward all that time. It is important to not take any arising tension personally, but to stay calm and level-headed, and to respond to problems in a mature and constructive way. At this point, only small changes can be achieved, but sometimes they can have a great effect.

Production Meetings

With the beginning of the rehearsal period, or shortly before that, a series of regular meetings, known as production meetings, commence. They will often be planned from the first day of rehearsals onwards and happen on a weekly basis. It is an opportunity to see the key professionals of the production team, such as the production manager, the director, the set designer and the lighting designer, and to address questions. Depending on the type of costumes and the size of production, there might be one or several meetings when representatives of the various costume departments join the conversation. The costume designer needs to ensure that they attend all meetings. On the day of the first production meeting, there is often the design presentation, potentially in the presence of the cast. This is a great opportunity for the designer to introduce themselves and to find out who are the other professionals.

Lighting

Ordinarily, technical rehearsals start with the lighting team installing the lighting bars and lights, known as rigging. What follows the rigging is the focusing of the lights. This will partly be happening with some of the performers present in the space. It is not unusual for performers to wear their costume at this point to give the lighting designer, director and costume designer a better idea of the final image.

This image shows areas of the stage of an opera house that are ordinarily hidden from the audience. Visible here are the lights rigged on a bar and stage weights on a trolley in the foreground. These are used to secure set pieces, for example.

GET-IN AND FIT-UP

Another team will start installing the set, which is called the set 'get-in' and 'fit-up'. This might happen simultaneously to the lighting or it might only overlap slightly. The technical manager, theatre manager and/or production manager and set designer will oversee this process. The technical manager is the professional who is in charge of managing the team of technicians and makes most of the decisions concerning the space, and health and safety regulations. Most concerns and issues need to be run by them. After the get-in and fit-up have been completed, the actors or performers and the director come in and start rehearsing. In the beginning of these rehearsals, the focus will be on using the set correctly and safely. Further lighting adjustments might be happening during this time.

DRESS REHEARSALS

There will be several full performance runs, of which at least one will be in full costume, hair and make-up. A rehearsal in costume is called 'dress rehearsal'. In most cases, it is the last rehearsal before the opening night and often takes place on the day of the performance or the day before. This rehearsal is expected to run in order and without stopping. The dress rehearsal will often be the only opportunity to film and photograph a production, so it is important to have all aspects of the show completed. Sometimes dress rehearsals are open to the public and, most of the time, there will be a small audience of internal staff watching it. After the opening of the show, the responsibility of the designer tends to end and is passed on to the wardrobe team. However, the wardrobe team will have started to rehearse quick changes during these final rehearsals and begin the process of maintenance.

IN OPERA

An opera production needs several additional rehearsals due to its complexity. Initial rehearsals will only be accompanied by the piano, instead of the whole orchestra. A full performance run might be beneficial at this stage to rehearse quick changes and scene transitions. These rehearsals tend to happen in a rehearsal room or, in many cases, spread out over several spaces, due to the sheer number of professionals involved. As rehearsals progress, the full orchestra needs to be integrated, which is a complex process. Some orchestras can consist of dozens of musicians. Often, there is also a choir, which can reach

ACT 1
Minotaur

ACT 1
Phaedra

Costume design by set and costume designer Takis for *Phaedra* (2007, by Hans Werner Henze, directed by Noa Naamat, 2019, ROH, London).

numbers close to a hundred. Rehearsals involving the orchestra and singers are often referred to as *sitzprobe*, which literally means rehearsing while sitting in a chair. It emphasizes that singers do not act out the scenes but rather practise their parts together with the members of the orchestra. It is advantageous for this rehearsal phase to move on to the stage in order to get an idea for the sound quality. These rehearsals are followed by those referred to as 'stage and orchestra', which involve the performers acting out the scenes on stage and, ideally, with the involvement of the set, props and key costumes. Toward opening night, there will be the need to rehearse in costume, hair and make-up.

WHEN THE WARDROBE TEAM TAKES OVER

To ensure that the costumes look as intended and as best as they can in every show, it is advisable that the designer or supervisor makes sure that the wardrobe team has all the information needed. This will be information on how the costumes are worn, for example, whether a shirt is tucked in or out, and on washing and caring instructions. In order to keep track of this information, and to archive it, the supervisor compiles it into one big file, known as the 'costume bible'. Smaller scale productions might require the designer to create a bible themselves. In some instances, this might be beneficial in case there are questions later on. Beyond relaying all necessary information to the wardrobe team in the form of a clear document, the costume bible becomes relevant in a couple of other scenarios, for example, if there is a change in wardrobe team members or the show travels to another theatre, where another wardrobe team will have to learn how to look after the costumes. The costume bible will also be necessary if a production is revived, especially after a long time. In larger theatres and opera houses, there can be a dedicated team to do this work, sometimes referred to as the 'costume revival department'. Members of this team fit costumes to the new performers and, if necessary, repair them or even remake those not usable any more.

Whether or not, and to what extent, a designer needs to be involved after the premiere of a show, depends on the type of contract and the expectations of the theatre, director or production

This is an example of the costume design and its realization by set and costume designer Takis for *Atomic Saloon* (2019, Spiegelworld, The Venetian Hotel and Casino, Las Vegas, directed by Cal McCrystal).

company. While rather uncommon, in some rare cases, the designer might be expected to oversee and even sometimes assist with some of the tasks after the show has opened. The designer is well advised to find out those details before accepting a job and be clear about the extent to which they are willing to get involved. The designer should really not be expected to assist the wardrobe team during the run of the show, but somehow sometimes it comes up in discussions or is even presumed.

REPERTORY THEATRE

Repertory theatre describes a type of programming in which successful stage productions are revived on a regular basis, often over years and decades. Particularly successful productions of stories such as *Alice in Wonderland* or the ballet *Swan Lake* and seasonal productions such as *The Nutcracker* are brought back on to the stage every year or couple of years, sometimes even a long time after their premiere. Set and costumes for these shows will have been stored somewhere to be re-used, if and when needed, and, therefore,

these shows neither require a new design, nor the designer to come back. That makes it much more cost-effective for a theatre and is one of the most common ways of securing revenue. The revival of costumes should be possible without the designer present but with the help of the costume bible. It is unusual to ask the designer back for this process, but they might want to see the show again to make sure the costumes are up to standard. In some cases, there might be a financial benefit from getting involved in this type of production, but this will have to be discussed when signing the contract.

A FEW DETAILS ON THE FILM AND TELEVISION PRODUCTION PROCESS

Film and television productions barely rely on rehearsals but on, potentially several, camera takes. They could be considered a form of rehearsing, only that they are recorded and potentially used in the end product. During the shooting of a film or TV series, the designer might want to

The costume realization is a complex process that can involve pattern-cutting, draping, fabric sampling and tailoring, as demonstrated here by costume designer and maker Sophie Ruth Donaldson for *Hansel and Gretel and the Witch Baba Yaga* (2017, written by Daniel Winder, directed by Amy Draper) and *Sumida River* (2021, Naohiko Umewaka).

be present and oversee the process, as much as they, and the rest of the team, deem it necessary. Availability can be a delicate position to navigate, as the designer will have many other responsibilities and prioritizing is not as straightforward. Their availability depends on the structure that is in place; for example, whether they have assistants and a supervisor, the size of the production and the locations of the workrooms and the costume store. In that respect, the shooting of a film does not differ from stage rehearsals.

On the film set, it is the costume standby team that not only gathers information and passes it on to the designer, but also addresses a lot of the challenges that might arise during filming. The standby and/or running wardrobe team need to be sufficiently briefed by the costume designer, who might be present at the beginning of a shoot when the costume appears for the first time. The designer will want to discuss the day with the costume standby but then might have to leave the set to get on with other tasks, such as preparing costumes for the following day, conducting fittings with actors or watching the footage from the previous day to review their work on-screen. If

time allows, however, the costume designer might spend a substantial amount of time watching the shooting of a film and attending to costume concerns.

After the shooting of a film has been completed, costumes will be returned. However, a situation can arise, and often does, where scenes need to be shot again and the same costumes are required again. That can lead to problems if this has not been accounted for. Professional costume-hire places offer the option to store costumes for a certain period of time should this situation arise.

THE COSTUME-MAKING PROCESS IN MORE DETAIL

Making costumes requires an enormous number and variety of skills, which are often not found in one maker but a team of makers with different specializations. Going into great detail of knowledge required to make a costume is beyond the scope of this book but a short overview will be outlined in this section. Some costume-makers work in a way whereby they create a costume from start to

Most costume departments, costume-makers and, certainly, pattern-cutters have a selection of basic patterns for shirts, trousers and dresses, which are called 'blocks'. They are very valuable and are often made of more robust material, such as card or thick paper, to ensure their longevity.

finish. In other contexts, the process is split into several steps carried out by different professionals. Depending on the costume, the designer or supervisor will find the right maker or team of makers. To be a great costume designer, it is not mandatory to master the various making skills. However, the more the designer knows about them, the more control they will have over the outcome of their designs. Expert knowledge will help the designer to communicate with the team of makers more effectively and, furthermore, be taken seriously when making demands, especially when they entail more work for the team. Different work contexts will require the designer to have knowledge of more or fewer making skills. Especially when starting out in fringe theatre and independent film-making, basic making skills might become essential, and basic knowledge of repairing and altering costumes will always be good to have.

Pattern-Cutting

One of the first steps, if not the first when making a costume, will be the creation of a pattern or the adaptation of an existing one, using a basic pattern, also known as the pattern block. The pattern of a garment is a two-dimensional drawing of a three-dimensional form. It is the basis of the costume and, therefore, absolutely crucial to the costume-making process. It allows to control the outcome of the costume to a minute level. Furthermore, it makes it possible to replicate the same costume infinite times, while allowing changes to be made to it, as and when needed. Being able to manipulate a pattern is crucial, first, because the performer's body might change shape over time and, second, the performer might need to be substituted at some point. This could, in some cases, require a total remake of the same costume in a different size. Furthermore, the same pattern might be the basis for hundreds of costumes of the same style and shape but worn by different performers of varying sizes and, potentially, in different fabrics and colours. A lot of costume designers have studied pattern-cutting and consider it immensely helpful to have a basic understanding of it at every stage of the design process. Furthermore, it enables the designer to grasp fundamental questions and, consequently, to communicate their ideas more effectively.

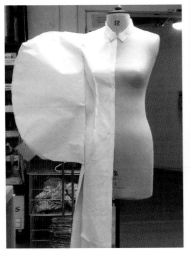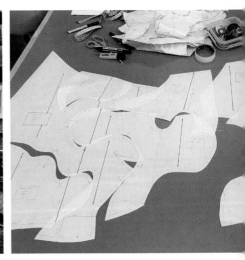

Pattern-cutting is an integral part of costume-making. It requires training and can be very complex, as demonstrated here by costume designer and maker Sophie Ruth Donaldson. Creative pattern-cutting requires a mannequin on to which pattern pieces can be mounted allowing further manipulation.

The most important tool when making a pattern is the curve ruler, of which there is a variety available and every pattern cutter has their own preference. It is also known as a pattern master or French curve. Some professionals import them from other countries because they want a very particular curve. Other basic tools are a pair of quality fabric scissors or a rotary cutter, tailor's chalk and the tracing wheel, which the maker uses to mark out lines; the latter is used in combination with chalk paper. A mannequin is also pretty much mandatory. It is irreplaceable when needing to test a pattern's functionality and translation into the three-dimensional form by pinning the pattern pieces on to it, for example, as seen in the photographs accompanying this text.

Depending on the training and the location, costume professionals use different pattern-cutting methods. It is common to combine a variety of methods and to include draping on the stand, a much more organic approach to making a pattern. Pattern-cutting requires training as well as practice and a technical as well as a creative mind. However, it might not be absolutely essential to undergo formal training. There are many books on pattern-cutting, online tutorials and a variety of short courses available that can assist a keen learner to gain basic knowledge, in fact on pretty much everything regarding costume construction. An apprenticeship with a tailor or choosing a specific module as part of a degree is advisable when a desire for much more comprehensive knowledge exists. When wanting to learn pattern-cutting, it is advisable to practise creating basic patterns, known as 'blocks', from scratch and then experiment with dart manipulation or sizing. It is also useful to buy patterns and study them, perhaps manipulate them into something new. It could be a successful way of learning more about pattern-cutting to follow the instructions of a book on draping. There are also plenty of free online tutorials available, ranging from basic pattern-cutting to more complex pattern tutorials, often referred to as creative pattern-cutting. It is worth considering contacting a cutter and enquiring for some shadowing work or work experience. Equally successful might be to look for an entry-level job in a costume-making studio, where it would be acceptable to ask questions, allowing some on-the-job experience to be gained.

At some point during the creation of the pattern, fabric will be sourced to commence with the

 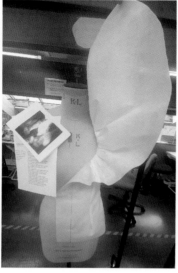  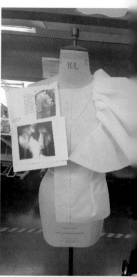

Creative pattern-cutting is a form of pattern cutting that departs from the basic block pattern, as demonstrated here by costume designer and maker Sophie Ruth Donaldson.

Pattern-cutting requires specialist tools, seen in this image, which shows the pattern-cutting process of costume designer and maker Sophie Ruth Donaldson.

Costume design and make for *Starchitects* (2019, Motionhouse) by costume designer Sophie Ruth Donaldson.

making. Not always, but very often, the choice of fabric will have an impact on the pattern, especially when it is a stretch material. This type of expert knowledge, however, is not required from a designer, unless they are a designer-maker and work in fields such as dance, as outlined earlier. Otherwise in such questions, the designer can rely on the maker's opinion or consult other experts, if unsure.

Tailoring

After the pattern has been made, the making of the costume can commence, starting with the cutting of fabric. Before this step, however, the fabric will have to be washed and ironed. Fabrics that have not been pre-washed often shrink slightly, so it is important to do this prior to cutting or the costume will not fit after it has been made and washed. It is also important that any major dyeing has happened before cutting, as this process heats the fabric and may also result in shrinkage. In some cases, it is useful to iron the fabric to examine the possibility of it shrinking. In all cases it needs to be ironed to prepare it for cutting. Some fabrics will not be washable or cannot be ironed. The cutter or maker should have a good understanding of the individual particularities of the various fabrics available. If unsure, testing on a sample of the same fabric is highly recommendable. Once sure, the fabric can be carefully spread out on a big table, the cutting table. The pattern will then need to be laid on top of the fabric. While doing so, any wrinkles need to be flattened out. Pattern pieces are cut out with a seam

allowance around them to allow for their sewing together. This can vary between 1 and 3cm, in some cases even more, to accommodate any alterations later on. Some cutters work with the seam-allowance already accounted for on their pattern pieces. Others will add it on when cutting out the fabric, by drawing the seam-allowance on to the fabric, using tailor's chalk. There are advantages and disadvantages to both methods and usually it depends on personal preference.

The next step is to begin the garment construction. Most pattern pieces will not only be sewn together but treated beforehand to prevent the fabric from fraying. This is usually the first step in the garment construction, which is achieved by using a special machine called an overlocker, which adds a 5–10mm protective seam along the edge of the fabric. Garment construction can be relatively straightforward or rather complex, depending on the complexity of the garment and method of the maker and/or tailor. Some makers begin with pinning the fabric pieces in order to sew them together. The order of the pieces that need sewing together plays a crucial role. Last, but not least, most garments require the adding of appropriate fastening and a substantial amount of hand-sewing.

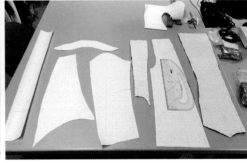

Pattern-cutting by costume designer and maker Frances Morris, who uses tailor's chalk to mark out necessary lines on the fabric. Many professional maker's studios and designers, too, use professional cutting tables. They tend to be larger and of above average height to accommodate the work while standing up. This can be anything between 90 and 120cm, and some tables are height-adjustable. This is an important detail, as leaning forwards repetitively will inevitably lead to back problems. Makers are under a lot of body strain and should try to do everything in their power to make their workstation safe.

Costume design and make by set and costume designer Bettina John for *Broken Dreams* (2019, Belinda Evangelica) (headpiece and beadwork by Anna Kompaniets).

can be pretty noisy but are a lot smoother and quicker, and are much stronger in comparison to the domestic machine. Industrial machines also need a special electric support. The other main difference is that industrial machines commonly only have one type of stitch, the straight stitch, and sometimes a zig-zag stitch. Domestic machines tend to have a much wider variety of stitches, including a stretch stitch. There are also both domestic and industrial overlockers available.

Specialist-Making, Textile and Surface Treatment

Most costumes require a lot more work than what has been laid out so far and the involvement of specialist makers will become necessary. These could be embroiderers, beaders, weavers or textile artists, who treat surfaces to make them appear in a certain way. The fact that costumes often have to undergo a special treatment in order to look old, worn or dirty, for example, is less obvious to people who do not work in costume. It is an important aspect to costume-making, as it supports the costume's function to tell a story. An epic war film, for example, that shows extensive fighting on the battlefield, will require an enormous number of professionals to dirty down the soldier's costumes. Without that final treatment, this scene would not be convincing at all. This work is mostly referred to as the 'breaking down' of costumes. The department responsible for this is often referred to as 'specialist textiles', and the roles within are known under titles such as dyers and agers, or surface and textile artists, depending on the location and industry. The making of some costumes, such as hats, costume props, armour, masks, corsets or tutus, will go straight to a specialist-maker, as they require a very different making process.

On the subject of sewing machines, it is useful to add that there are two types of sewing machines, additional to the overlooker, which is a different machine altogether. There is the domestic sewing machine, a relatively small machine that can easily be set up in any space. The other type is the industrial sewing machine, which can vary in size, but tends to be a lot bigger. It comes with a table attached to it and is, therefore, a lot heavier and requires a lot more space. These machines

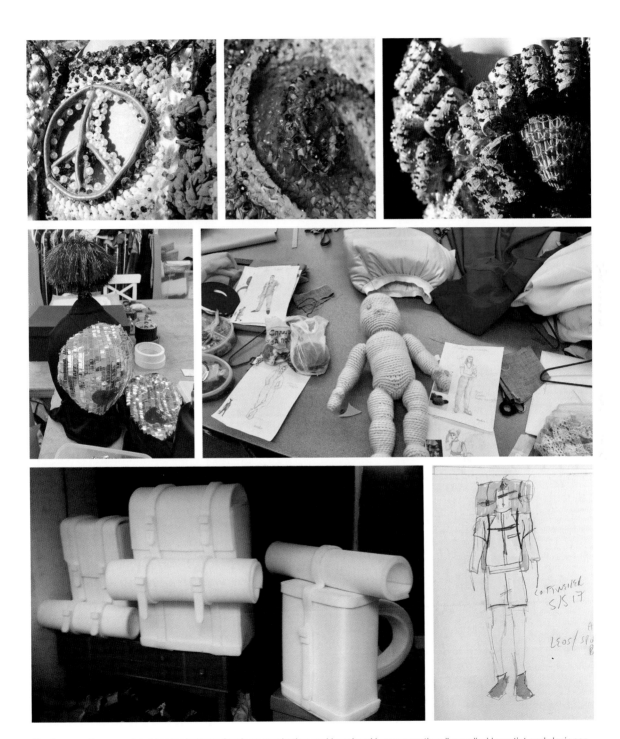

Top images: A range of making techniques (such as crocheting and beadwork) unconventionally applied by artist and designer Anna Kompaniets. Rarely using a sewing machine, Kompaniets developed exceptional hand-sewing skills. ALLA SANDERS
Middle left: Masks by designer and maker Sophie Ruth Donaldson for *Stunners* (2019, Tamar & Jo).
Middle right: Props making by the TUZ costume department in Perm, Russia for *Alice in Wonderland* (2020, directed by Michael Hunt). A costume team can potentially consist of dozens of specialist makers such as knitters, beaders, costume prop-makers, weavers and many more.
Bottom: Costume prop-making by Sophie Ruth Donaldson for *I'll See It When I Believe It* (2018, Theo Clinkard).

Broken-down and aged costume by set and costume designer Bettina John for Alberich of *Rheingold* (2019, The Arcola Theatre, directed by Julia Burbach, photograph by Lidia Crisafulli). The costume professionals responsible for this work are called breakdown artists, agers or dyers and their department is sometimes referred to as specialist textiles. Professionals working in this field often have a background in textiles or textile design. However, small- and medium-scale productions might require the designer to take on some of these tasks.

Breaking Down Costumes

Methods to break down costumes vary, sometimes greatly, depending on the production and context. Different professionals can have very different methods, of which some can be very complex and others quite simple. Distressing a garment requires a combination of washing, to help break down the fabric, painting and working it over with tools, like sandpaper; it is time-intensive work. To make costumes appear dirty, for example, they could be partly dyed and partly painted, using various types of paint, such as specially manufactured canned spray-paint or airbrush paint; acrylic and other types of paint could work too. In order to appear convincing, various layers of paint might need to be applied in combination with distressing the material. Some professionals prefer using tea, beetroot, coffee and even mud and grass to dirty down costumes. Any method applied needs to be considered regarding its permanency. In most cases, costumes will have to be washed and ironed, which might remove some of the paint effects. To achieve garments appearing old and worn, certain parts, such as the elbow, knee, collar, cuff and pocket areas need to be distressed.

Common tools to use for the breaking down of materials are the wire brush, cheese-grater and scissors to fray edges and score and tear the fabric. Brushes will be used to apply paint and powder. Sandpaper is irreplaceable when needing to manipulate surfaces, for example, soften it or working paint into it and to wear down fibres. Apart from various types of paint, other substances, such as glycerine, to make an area appear shiny might be applied. Vaseline can be used to help dirt stick on to a surface and is particularly useful to make areas such as cuffs and collars appear worn. Specially developed blood paints with varying degree of thickness and other useful, ready-to-use tools, such as the grease stick, are available to purchase from special suppliers, such as a 'theatrical chandler'.

EXERCISES

Exercise 1: Fitting and Styling

Find a volunteer, for example, a friend, partner or family member, who will feel comfortable with this exercise. Use a selection of your clothes or a selection of garments your volunteer is happy to provide. No damage will be done to them. Ask your volunteer to put on your first combination of garments selected from what is available. Determine their fit on your volunteer. Are they too tight or too loose? What can you do to improve any problems? Observe how the garments behave in movement. Determine the combination of garments and whether they suit your volunteer. Experiment with different methods on how to wear these particular garments, such as rolling up the sleeves or trousers, or adding a scarf or hat. Experiment with different combinations. Add a theme to this experimentation, such as formal wear, casual wear, a winter walk wear and so on. Make notes and repeat this with a couple more combinations.

Exercise 2: Breaking Down Fabrics

Find a garment or piece of fabric that you can use for this exercise. Cut it into smaller pieces. Prepare a container that can withstand near to boiling water, which is what you will need to use for this exercise. Add one or two bags of tea. Add the first piece of fabric. Experiment with the time you leave the fabric in and the strength of the tea. Try other readily available substances, such as coffee, beetroot and ordinary paint, and experiment with their potential to achieve believable ageing and staining effects. Using scissors and a metal brush, for example, break down the fabric in various places. Experiment with the intensity with which you use these tools.

Exercise 3: Understanding a Garment

Find an old garment you would otherwise take to the charity shop. You will need a pair of small scissors or an unpicker. Unpick the garment and spread all parts on to a table. This allows you to see the basic construction of the garment and gives you a starting point to make a pattern yourself. You need paper for the next part, which is to draw around the edges of the fabric pieces. Take the piece off the paper and examine the result. Repeat this with the other pieces.

7

HOW TO BREAK INTO THE INDUSTRY AND SURVIVE

Carving out a career in the arts can be a complex negotiation of a lot of different factors, particularly a career as a costume designer. Not only are there many different contexts for a costume designer to work in, but also an enormous amount of specialization. It does not help that the day-to-day work and the skill-set of a costume designer is not fully understood or communicated effectively. This chapter sheds some light on the enumerable pathways an early career costume professional can choose from and the challenges they will have to face.

COSTUME TRAINING

Finding the right pathway is an individual journey and it is never absolutely clear in the beginning how a career will develop. Some individuals might find that they only need to take a few courses and then find a low-entry job that enables them to start learning while already earning money and working in the industry. Other individuals might need to take several courses, or study a degree, take work placements and apply for many jobs, until they are finally offered their

OPPOSITE: The professional costume designer will spend many hours on selecting images and finding the best solutions to present them. This page shows one of infinite solutions by set and costume designer Bettina John for *Alice in Wonderland* (2019/20, a new adaptation of the story by Lewis Carroll by Ilya Gubin for The Theatre for Young Spectators (TUZ), Russia, directed by Michael Hunt, photographs by Roman Gorbatovskogo).

first one. There is no formula and no set pathway with a guaranteed outcome.

There seems to be an understanding amongst some individuals that the trajectory to becoming a costume professional needs to lead through university. However, there are enumerable other pathways to becoming a costume professional, such as traineeships and apprenticeships with companies, academies, schools and organizations. It is not impossible to learn on the job. Most professionals will tell you that they learnt their most valuable lessons on the job. It is important to understand the difference between studying for a university degree and undergoing training and practising and learning on a job. If there is an interest in experimenting and studying a field in more depth, then university is the right place. University requires students to write about their work, eventually leading to the final written work, the dissertation. However, if there is the desire to learn about the actual profession and industry, and gain work experience, then turning straight to the organization of interest might be the better and more effective choice.

The following list will give an idea of the training available to aspiring costume professionals. However, it does not presume to be exhaustive, nor can it be more specific, as the theatre and educational landscape is ever-changing. It is merely a list aimed toward showing those individuals with the desire to work within costume how many options there are available and that nothing should stop them from becoming what they want to be.

- A traineeship with a production company (potentially paid)
- A traineeship with a costume organization (potentially paid).
- A traineeship with a costume department in an institution, a drama or dance school or in a producing theatre (potentially paid).
- A traineeship with a costume studio or design studio (potentially paid).
- An apprenticeship with a tailor (potentially paid).
- Online and on-site short courses at universities or academies that offer a wide range of courses, such as an introduction to costume design, pattern-cutting, basic and advanced sewing skills, embroidery, textile design, tutu-making, wig-making and many more (the cost for these courses can vary tremendously).
- Similar courses offered by not-for-profit organizations, community centres, professional studios or privately by individual tutors and professionals.
- Diplomas at colleges.
- Bachelor or master's degrees at universities and colleges (this tends to be a rather expensive choice, but bursaries might be available for a handful of eligible candidates).
- Getting work at entry level (paid).
- Finding work placements/internships (paid or unpaid).
- Shadowing professionals (mostly unpaid, but expenses should be expected to be covered).

The introduction to theatre, and costume specifically, might be as early as primary or secondary school. It might be the case that a child is involved in a Christmas play or joins a youth theatre. It is through educational institutions that most young people will be introduced to theatre and all its aspects, such as costume. Therefore, those institutions have a responsibility for representing all aspects of the performing arts in the best way possible, including that of costume design. Whether it is a primary or secondary school, a college, a youth theatre, a community centre or, later on, a university or an academy, it is there where individuals gain an understanding of what costume design is and it is there, where misconceptions could start forming. A simple and seemingly small point about the title of a course or module and what is actually being taught can indeed have a great effect on the understanding of a whole profession. Therefore, the difference between costume as opposed to costume design should be observed. Costume describes the whole field and encompasses many different roles, whereas costume design describes one role within the industry.

Other Costume Roles

It is important to understand that becoming a costume designer is not the only option aspiring costume professionals have. The field of costume offers a wide range of roles, as this book illustrates at various points. Each of these roles requires a particular skill-set and training. A costume team has one costume designer and sometimes hundreds of other costume professionals realizing the costume design and ensuring the smooth running of the department. It is worth considering if any of these roles might be more suitable. Furthermore, the chances to get offered costume design work, straight after having completed training, are fairly slim. Most, if not all, costume professionals have gone through a wide range of costume roles before starting to design. Some professionals set out to become designers and then find another, much more suitable role along the way. It is important to keep an open mind and, if necessary, adapt to new circumstances and challenges that come with them. This might mean to potentially slightly shift career, possibly work in a specific region, with specific groups of people, in a specific niche, or offer a specific skill-set and retrain for it.

English National Opera Costume Department.

WHAT HAPPENS AFTER TRAINING

After having completed university or training, it is common to start at entry level and gain experience, before a chance to assist a designer and eventually a chance to design a small-scale show will arise. Particularly in large-scale productions, there are plenty of different opportunities for aspiring costume professionals. It is worth applying for any costume role available, although the enormous competition makes it difficult for graduates with no work experience to be successful, especially when there are many more experienced professionals looking for work. Larger theatres, production companies or makers' studios have often more opportunities to take on early career professionals.

With a bit of networking, good skills, a good attitude and willingness to help, it should be possible to find a costume position. Depending on the skill-set of the early career professional, other roles might be available to them, such as a costume technician role in a costume department of a theatre or production company, a drama school or costume-makers' studio. However, these positions can require a high degree of sewing skills and a knowledge of how to alter costumes, do repairs and conduct fittings. In some cases, pattern-making skills are necessary. The more skills the early career professional can offer, the more likely it will be that they will find an entry position within costume. In the first few years, getting to know the industry and building relationships will play a significant role and determine much of the following career.

Internships

Depending on the financial situation of the early career designer, there are several options available after training has been completed. It might be an option for some to seek out a work placement.

Opportunities can be found by looking through notice boards, signing up to newsletters, searching company websites or writing to the place of interest directly. The industry is welcoming to early career costume professionals wanting to gain work experience. Unpaid opportunities, however, are controversial, but most designers, working successfully in the industry today, will have taken unpaid work at various stages of their career. It is important to weigh up the benefits with potential exploitation and damage done to the industry and other professionals who are not in the position to take unpaid work. Opinions around this keep changing with the political and social landscape of the time, and talking to peers and professionals about specific situations is advisable. An opportunity to 'shadow' a designer, which is a form of work placement that is the least formal of all opportunities, can be especially helpful for those who do not have enough experience or skills yet, or who are not even entirely sure about this as a career choice.

Assisting

One of the directions a costume designer can choose to take is assisting a more senior costume designer, while taking low-paid design opportunities to establish themselves as a designer in their own right. There is one caveat: within the theatre industry, the role of assistant costume designer is less common; instead, there is the role of supervisor, which is a slightly different role, as explained earlier. In film and television, the assistant costume designer is a much more common role, and some large-scale projects will even employ several assistant costume designers.

MAKING A LIVING AS A DESIGNER
Adopting Other Costume Roles

One option to increase and/or ensure a basic income, alongside working as a designer, is to adopt another role within costume, such as supervising, costume-making, pattern-cutting, dressing, costume alteration and repairs. Not only are most of these skills part of the costume training anyway, but also a lot of designers enjoy them as much as they enjoy designing. There are opportunities, especially within dance, where costume designers are hired to design, make and take on other responsibilities. This combination gives costume designers a chance to make a living, while also designing and building a portfolio.

Teaching

Whether costume-related subjects or any other subjects, teaching can also sit comfortably alongside designing costume, but again, this requires a certain skill-set and personality, and is not for everybody.

Diversifying

To diversify one's practice and look outside of film, television and theatre and into fields such as fashion, styling and advertisement could also be helpful. Finding work of this kind could be equally challenging, but, for some, it might be a natural way of artistic expression and achievable to compile a suitable portfolio or connect to the necessary people, which is often the more useful task. In some cases, the aspiring costume designer might already operate in a circle of people who could assist in getting these jobs.

Supporting Low-Paid Design Roles with Part-Time Work

Another option to support one's living is to work in roles unrelated to costume design. This could be anything from waiting tables to admin jobs or even a job that has been practised before deciding to become a costume designer. There are

Testing costume design against the set design is an important step in the production process. These images show Cinema 4D computer-generated designs by stage and costume designer Chiara Stephenson for *Starry Messenger* (2019, directed by Sam Yates).

many professionals within costume who have had a completely different career before they decided to want to change. This is a way to ensure a living and puts the designer in a position where they can accept costume design work that is either low paid or even unpaid.

Receiving Financial Support

Applying for grants, bursaries and competitions is yet another way to support a costume practice, especially when a more radical direction toward costume art, sometimes also referred to as wearable art and/or sculpture, has been taken. It might be worthwhile for the costume designer to explore the possibility of private support or crowdfunding through online platforms such as *Patreon*, where a community of friends and benefactors might be willing to support a costume designer for a certain period of time. Quite a few early career costume designers need to rely on support, and it is a great advantage to the designer to be inventive when looking for ways to find it.

BUILDING RELATIONSHIPS

One of the most important skills to develop for this career is connecting with other professionals. Most of the time, personal connections or a recommendation from a trusted acquaintance, colleague or friend is necessary to be seriously considered for a position. Often surprisingly, this recommendation can be obtained relatively easily with a little inventiveness and the right attitude. While reaching out for the stars is always worth a try, investigating the team surrounding the superstar, an assistant, for example, can sometimes be more worthwhile. It might be easier to establish a contact with another member of their team, than approaching the top designer directly. Simply researching how a particular team is structured, who its members are and what their roles entail, can be greatly insightful. What any of these suggestions have in common is showing evidence of genuine interest. As long as this can be demonstrated when approaching somebody, it will likely be successful. Simple details such as using the correct name and position, knowing a little bit about the specific role, understanding what a company is about, showing interest in the work they do and connecting it to the reasons for approaching them, are fundamental and really make a difference.

Partnering with a Set Designer

In the British theatre industry, a lot of designers take on both roles, that of the costume and the set designer. However, some designers prefer to only design the set or can foresee when being offered the role as set and costume designer that they will not have enough time and resources to take on both of these roles. There lies a great opportunity for a costume designer to step in, maybe even build up a permanent relationship with a set designer. In other countries, it is a much more

Stage design by stage and costume designer Chiara Stephenson for *Björk II Cornucopia II the Shed NYC* (2019, Björk). Although engaged as the set designer for this show, Stephenson's process considers the costume design (Olivier Rousteing and Iris van Herpen) in her computer-generated stage designs. In the performing arts, the human body, in relation to the space it finds itself in, plays a tremendous role. Without the body, the performance space cannot fully be understood.

common practice to separate these two roles and it might be worth looking beyond the boundaries of the UK. Furthermore, the bigger the production and budget, the more likely it is for these two roles to be separate.

Networking

There are many ways to connect to people, especially with the various digital tools available today. Whether it is the setting up and running of a social media account, the joining of professional groups or the building up and looking after individual relationships, each of these options can be extremely successful in making and keeping connections. It all depends on the context and the quality of the engagement. In recent years, social media has somewhat surpassed the making of connections over a drink in a bar. Some people might even go so far and question whether this has ever been an effective way. Certainly, it depends on the individual. What social media can assist with, extremely well, is making connections across the world. It has also helped tremendously to lower the barriers that hierarchies had established. Currently,

it is possible to follow an individual designer on social media and establish a direct contact with them that way.

It is important to keep in mind that connecting to somebody does not have to have the specific aim in mind of being offered a job. Instead, it should be more about building a network of people in which a genuine interest exists. Operating in such a network will eventually present opportunities. Networking is an exercise that is most effective when consistently happening in the background. It is most successful when it feels natural, becomes a second language; for some people that is a challenging task. Networking through social media has helped many to overcome those initial challenges but a shift in the understanding of what networking means can help those that still struggle. Networking means connecting to people and that is what it should be. This outlook will help to make it more enjoyable, as it brings it back to authenticity and honesty.

It might be a good experience, especially when starting out in costume, to join and sign up to a variety of relevant newsletters and groups online. Social media offers plenty of open groups and forums specifically designed to support costume

These portfolios are examples of an A4 and A3 landscape format and an A2 portrait format, commonly used among designers to show their work to potential collaborators or submit it into competitions.

professionals. There might be a more tightly defined group that could be joined, a regional one, one that supports women or specific minorities, niche work or a specific interest within costume. There are also more widely defined groups, such as costume for film and television, theatre or dance, opera or music. A lot of theatres, organizations or unions offer platforms for designers and directors to connect. They might organize so-called speed-dating events, workshops and offer discounted tickets to see shows, for example. They might offer support and mentoring and help to connect their members. Local theatre groups or amateur theatre groups might also be a great way to meet like-minded people and find opportunities. Last but not least, it is worth investigating which friends work in the industry and would be willing to help.

HELPFUL TOOLS TO DEMONSTRATE SKILLS

Connecting to people and building relationships play a crucial role in finding work and building a career. Equally fundamental, however, is producing excellent work and developing a successful format to present it. A very high percentage of graduates, apprentices and trainees have developed a great talent and demonstrate all the other relevant skills, but if they are not visible and their work is not made accessible, they will not be seen.

Portfolio

The basic tool to present work is the portfolio. Portfolios have been used by creatives for hundreds of years and are still irreplaceable. What has been changing over time though is the form and format that portfolios can be worked into. It is remarkable just how many options there are available today. At a later stage in a designer's career, a portfolio might be less relevant and their reputation or their collaborators more important. A lot of situations might require a website or social media account, rather than the traditional portfolio. The portfolio does not have to be a book with drawings and photographs; nonetheless the classic type of a portfolio is still a great choice and could be useful at various points throughout the designer's career. Websites, social media, pdfs and other digital tools can also be used as portfolios and are often geared that way. Each of these tools has their pros and cons and suit certain scenarios better than others; most of the time, professionals today use a selection, if not all, of them. Not only does this mean a lot of time will go into creating and maintaining, adjusting and updating them, but it can also be a bit overwhelming sometimes.

A designer will inevitably suit a specific context due to their approach, aesthetic and work track record. However, within that lies a potential to adjust a portfolio to suit a slightly different context. Determining what is relevant to include in a portfolio can sometimes feel like an impossible task but is crucial to a successful portfolio. For that reason, it is important to ask for feedback from colleagues and friends. Some elements in a portfolio will help to convey an essence of the designer's work and ideas, while other elements demonstrate certain skills and achievements. Every element of a portfolio tells something about the professional, their work and their personality.

Online Presence

How professionals present themselves online, as well as in real life, is incredibly important. Websites, social media and numerous other online tools are not only available to professionals today but are also, to some extent, essential to use and maintain. The successful presentation of a designer's talent on their social media account, for example, is increasingly helpful when approaching another professional or applying for a position. It has become the norm to research somebody online before considering any further steps. A great alternative to the personal website are talent showcase platforms, such as *Behance* or *Cargocollective*, which promote a variety of talent working in a particular industry. This option is a lot simpler than creating a website and sometimes it might be the better choice, depending on the field and scene in which the designer is operating. It requires as little as registering and setting up a profile.

When facing the daunting task of creating an online presence, an enormous number of decisions need to be made and often they are about fundamental questions, such as 'who am I?' or 'what are my values?' and 'goals', not to mention the sometimes-technical challenges. There are many resources available to help in answering these questions. For those that are interested, there is also a lot of information obtainable online, advising on how to run a social media account successfully. There are many tricks to learn, such as the best times to post and what about, what extra tools to use, the most successful images and how to edit or what to write alongside them. While it always comes down to individual choices, there are rules that can be followed until a more personal approach can be developed. Other social media platforms that are less image-centred, such as Twitter, could also be utilized to great effect. They can assist in joining relevant conversations with other professionals, to find out about opportunities and to get the latest news and maybe a bit of gossip. Being up to date with what is happening in the scene can be very helpful when aspiring to be part of it.

CV and Covering Letter

Depending on the scenario and context, the CV and covering letter can be of great importance. In some scenarios, however, they might be less significant. In any case, it is advisable to have an up-to-date CV prepared. The CV might well be the reason to invite an applicant to an interview but from that point onwards it is the portfolio, personality and interaction that will make the difference. In the creative industry, in particular, there is no formula to a successful CV. It needs to be tailored to the situation, company and job description. Most importantly, the CV needs to demonstrate the relevant skills and requirements. It should be kept simple and clear, easy to read and as short as possible. What form this eventually take, has proven as complex as it can be surprising. There are a lot of specific online tutorials and resources available on this subject, which are well worth looking through.

The covering letter, or any less formal version of this introductory and motivational text, plays a very important role in building a career and is incredibly relevant at all career stages. It cannot be stressed enough how important a well written and engaging letter is in getting somebody's attention. It can literally make or break a relationship. One of the most basic, and actually the simplest, rules is to pay attention. That starts with getting the name and facts right and knowing why to approach this particular individual or apply for a role. It is important to truly care about the person and company and their work. A covering letter can be more influential than a CV, at least in this industry. However, the more formal the opportunities are, the more formal the approach has to be.

STAYING RELEVANT AND FURTHERING SKILLS

Today more than ever, it is a constant effort to stay relevant and to adapt to new circumstances, whether this is new technology, new forms of theatre, new channels to show the work, new ways of reaching an audience or, not least, finding new subject matter. When building a career as a costume designer, strategic thinking will be required at all stages. Whether starting out or being an established designer, looking into competitions, applying for awards or taking part in exhibitions are great ways to get work seen, potentially allowing a move into slightly different sectors of the industry or another one altogether. Furthermore, it is a chance for the designer to rethink their approach and processes applied thus far. Taking part in such opportunities can be a way to move a career forward and to develop on an artistic, as well as a personal, level. When feeling disconnected with the work that has been pursued for a few years, it might be time for a personal project or a project that sparks great interest and enthusiasm. If self-led work does not seem like an option, a short course or additional training, which are offered in abundance, might be the answer. Not only do most universities and academies offer a great variety of courses, the internet seems to produce more and more learning content, tutorials or so-called masterclasses.

PRACTICAL THINGS TO KNOW

There are a few steps designers can take that could help a career and make navigating working life a bit easier, starting with knowing what to charge for a job. While organizations such as unions publish minimum and average fees for designers regularly, sadly that does not mean it will be possible to always get these amounts. However, it is always worth challenging low-pay scenarios. A good starting point is to keep track of the hours spent on a project and multiply those by the average hourly income in the region. The level of experience a professional can offer plays a crucial role in how much an hourly pay can be. Most designers, however, are offered a flat fee and either take this or leave it. Depending on the stage of the designer's career, there is more or less room for negotiation. It is crucial to be realistic with the employer or recruiter, often the producer, about the amount of work that can be expected for a certain amount of money and to demonstrate this by breaking it down to an hourly rate. Most professionals involved in a theatre production do not know exactly how much work and time a designer actually invests in certain aspects of a show, which is why communicating this regularly and clearly is very important. This might not only help with the fee, but also with an understanding of what is, and is not, achievable.

A lot of designers try to find an agent when they think they have reached a certain level, or may be offered representation, who then will give support in these matters. It is not mandatory to a successful career as a designer, but in many situations it can help. Unlike the common understanding, having an agent does not necessarily mean an increase in work offers. However, an agency can increase the chances to meet other professionals by introducing clients to each other and setting up meetings, potentially opening doors for collaborations. If an agent is not an option, it is always worth considering joining unions, organizations and support groups that are available. There is support for every career stage and profession. In exchange for a small membership fee, unions offer professionals support when encountering unlawful or immoral practices and can intervene, if necessary involving relevant authorities. Most memberships come with certain extras such as insurances and access to mentoring, groups and valuable information.

FORM, GENRE AND INDUSTRY-SPECIFIC INFORMATION

The film and theatre industries offer a variety of entry roles for costume professionals but for aspiring costume designers, film and television have currently more opportunities to offer. While in the past, at least in the UK, the route to film had often been via the theatre industry, most graduates enter the film industry now directly, most often through companies such as the BBC and producers such as Netflix or Amazon. The various roles within the costume team can differ slightly from industry to industry. This can be particularly confusing when trying to decide what role to apply for. The role of the designer, however, is very similar across the industries and only varies due to the size and nature of the production.

The number of designs that will have to be delivered and subsequently overseen in the making of an opera, musical theatre and large-scale feature film production, can be substantially bigger than for a mid-scale or small-scale production. That means the designer will either have assistants or gets much more support from their costume supervisor and team. A designer has at least one, if not two, assistant costume designers when working on a large-scale film, or indeed a large-scale television production. In theatre and opera, that role will most often be filled with the supervisor and their assistants.

The size of budgets can differ greatly across the various industries, which has affected the way industries are structured. Film production, especially blockbuster production, ordinarily has much larger budgets than any other production. However, film too, is produced with low budgets, known as a micro-budget, which can be up to £150,000 in the UK. Many television series work with small budgets, while achieving great results. The difference in budgets, which can be pretty substantial, will undoubtedly impact a production though, especially the number of professionals involved, technology used and resources available.

Another difference to point out is that the various industries are organized in different ways, first and foremost the different hours and timeframes. While a theatre designer will work on several productions at the same time and their turnaround will be relatively quick, ranging from two years to just a few weeks, in film, the average shooting time can be far longer, requiring the designer to commit for a longer period of time. When working on a feature film, a designer will most likely not have the time to do many other projects. The shooting of a film can go on for months and the days can easily exceed twelve hours, starting as early as 6am. This is rather unusual for the theatre industry, where the days start between 8 and 10am.

RESOURCES

LIBRARIES

Westminster Library: www.westminster.ac.uk/current-students/studies/library-and-study-spaces

National Art library: www.vam.ac.uk/info/national-art-library/

British Library: www.bl.uk

University of the Arts (UAL) libraries: www.arts.ac.uk/students/library-services

City of London Barbican and Community libraries: www.barbican.org.uk/your-visit/during-your-visit/library

Rotherhithe Picture Research Library: www.sandsfilms.co.uk/rotherhithe-picture-research-library.html

New York Public Library for the Performing Arts: www.nypl.org

National Archives at New York City: www.archives.gov/nyc

Center for Brooklyn History: www.brooklynhistory.org

Kunstbibliothek Berlin: www.smb.museum/museen-einrichtungen/kunstbibliothek/home

Deutsche Nationalbibliothek (German National Library): www.dnb.de/DE/Home/home_node.html

Van Gogh Museum: www.vangoghmuseum.nl/en

Rijksmuseum Research Library: https://library.rijksmuseum.nl/

Media and Information Centre: www.zhdk.ch/en/miz

The NEBIS network: www.nebis.ch/en/frontpage

LADA Live Art Development Agency: www.thisisliveart.co.uk

ONLINE IMAGE ARCHIVES

Victoria & Albert Museum Images: www.vandaimages.com

British Library images online: https://imagesonline.bl.uk

The National Archives (UK): www.nationalarchives.gov.uk

The Prints and Photographs Online Catalogue (PPOC), The Library of Congress in Washington, DC: http://www.loc.gov/pictures/about/

Manchester Local Image Collection: https://images.manchester.gov.uk

Greater Manchester Lives: www.gmlives.org.uk

Welcome Collection Image Archive: https://wellcomecollection.org/works

Granger Historical Picture Archive: www.granger.com

The Getty Research Institute: www.getty.edu/research/tools/photo

The National Archives Catalogue for Pictures (USA): www.archives.gov

Victorian Picture Library: http://www.victorianpicturelibrary.com

The John Bright Collection: www.thejohnbrightcollection.co.uk

Tate Images and Tate Archive: www.tate.org.uk/art/archive

COSTUME-HIRE COMPANIES

ABC Costume Hire Ltd., Hertfordshire: https://abccostumehire.co.uk

Academy Costumes, London: www.academycostumes.co.uk

Angels, London: www.angels.co.uk

Bristol Costume Hire, London: www.bristolcostumeservices.com

Cosprop, London: www.cosprop.com

Costume Rentals Corporation, LA, USA: https://costumerentalscorp.com

Eastern Costume Inc, LA, USA: www.easterncostume.com

Foxtrot Costume and Props Ltd, London: www.foxtrotcostumeandprops.co.uk

Motion Picture Costume, Burbank, California, USA: www.motionpicturecostumeco.com

National Theatre London Costume Hire, London: www.nationaltheatre.org.uk/costume-and-props-hire

NBC Universal Costume Department, NY | Chicago, USA: http://stage.universal.filmmakersdestination.com/production-services/costume-department/

Palace Costume, LA, USA: www.palacecostume.com

Peris Costume, Madrid: https://periscostumes.com/en/home

Prangsta Costumiers, London: www.prangsta.co.uk

TDF Costume Collection, NY, USA: www.tdf.org/nyc/30/tdf-costume-collection

United American Costume, LA, USA: www.united-american.com

Western Costume Company, LA, USA: www.wccsupplystore.com

FURTHER READING, WATCHING AND LISTENING

Period Costume-Making, Pattern-Cutting and History of Fashion

Janet Arnold pattern books:

Patterns of Fashion 1 (the Cut and Construction of Women's Clothing, 1660–1860) (Wace, 1964; Macmillan, 1972; revised metric edition: Drama Books, 1977)

Patterns of Fashion 2: Englishwomen's Dresses and Their Construction c. 1860–1940 (Wace, 1966; Macmillan 1972; revised metric edition: Drama Books, 1977)

Perukes and Periwigs, National Portrait Gallery (A booklet on the development of wig styles in paintings at the National Portrait Gallery) (Her Majesty's Stationery Office, 1970)

A Handbook of Costume (A Guide to the Primary Sources for Costume Study) (Macmillan 1973; reprinted 1978)

Patterns of Fashion (The Cut and Construction of Clothes for Men and Women 1560–1620) (Macmillan,1985; revised edition 1986)

Queen Elizabeth's Wardrobe Unlock'd (W. S. Maney and Son Ltd, Leeds, 1988)

A study of the clothing of Queen Elizabeth I based on portraits, surviving inventories of the Wardrobe of Robes, and other original documents.

Patterns of Fashion 4 (The Cut and Construction of Linen Shirts, Smocks, Neckwear, Headwear and Accessories for Men and Women c. 1540–1660) (London, Macmillan, November 2008)

Nora Waugh pattern books:

Corsets and Crinolines (Theatre Art Books, 1954; revised edition Routledge 2017)

The Cut of Men's Clothes: 1600–1900 (Taylor & Francis Inc., 1987)

The Cut of Women's Clothes: 1600–1930 (Faber & Faber, 1994)

Aldrich, Winifred, *Metric Pattern-Cutting* (John Wiley & Sons; 1976, revised 5th edition 2008)

Aldrich, Winifred, *Metric Pattern-cutting for Women's Wear*, (Wiley, 96th edition, 2015)

Fischer, Annette and Gobin, Kiran, *Construction for Fashion Design*, (Bloomsbury Visual Arts, 2nd edition, 2017)

Malcom-Davies, J, *The Tudor Tailor* (Pavilion Books, 2006)

Nakamichi, Tomoko, *Pattern Magic* (Laurence King Publishing, 2010)

Thursfield, Sarah, *The Medieval Tailors Assistant* (The Crowood Press, 2015)

Tiramani, Jenny and North, Susan, *Seventeenth-Century Women's Dress Patterns: Book 1 and 2* (V&A Publishing, illustrated edition, 2011; updated 2013)

Sewing

Digest Complete Guide to Sewing (The Reader's Digest, 1st edition 1978; updated 2003)

Shaeffer, Claire B., *Couture Sewing Techniques* (Taunton Press Inc., 1st edition 1993; updated 2011)

Draping

Kiisel, Karolyn, *Draping: The Complete Course* (Laurence King Publishing, 1st edition 1881; updated 2013 and 2020)

History of Fashion

Cumming, Valerie, *Visual History of Costume Accessories* (Batsford Ltd, 1st edition, 1998)

Cunnington, C., Willet and Phillis, *History of Underclothes* (Cunnington, 1951)

Leventon, Melissa, *What People Wore When – A Complete Illustrated History of Costume from Ancient Times to the Nineteenth Century for Every Level of Society* (1st edition Book, 2008)

Schoeffler, O. E., *Esquire Men's Fashion of the 20th Century* (McGraw-Hill, 1st edition, 1973)

Schwabe, Randolph, *A Short History of Costume and Armour 1066–1800* (David & Charles, 1972)

Sichel, Marion, *History of Women's Costume* (Chelsea House Publications, 1990)

Styles, John, *The Dress of the People: Everyday Fashion in Eighteenth-Century England* (Yale University)

On Fabric and Textiles

Baugh, Gail, *The Fashion Designer's Textile Directory: The Creative Use of Fabrics in Design* (Barron's Educational Series, 2011)

Baugh, Gail, *The Fashion Designer's Textile Directory: A Guide to Fabrics' Properties, Characteristics, and Garment* (Barron's Educational Series, 2011)

Hallett, Clive and Johnston, Amanda, *Fabric for Fashion: The Complete Guide: Natural and Man-made Fibres* (Laurence King Publishing, illustrated, 2014)

More on Design

Bicat, Tina, *Costume and Design for Devised and Physical Theatre* (The Crowood Press, 2012)

Clancy, Deirdre, *Designing Costume for Stage and Screen* (Batsford Ltd, 2014)

Hywel Davies, *Fashion Designers' Sketchbooks Two* (Laurence King, Illustrated, 2013)

Jory, Marcia Dixcy, *Ingenue in White* (Smith & Kraus, 2003)

McAssey, Jacqueline and Buckley, Clare, *Basics: Fashion Design 08: Styling* (AVA Publishing, 2011)

SOCIETY OF BRITISH THEATRE DESIGNERS PUBLICATIONS:
Available from the website of the SBTD:
www.theatredesign.org.uk/exhibitions/

Make Believe (2015)
Transformation & Revelation (2011)
Collaborators: UK Design for Performance (2007)

Scholarly Discourse on Costume and Theatre

Intellect Books, Studies in Costume & Performance (Journal), (first published in 2016; Editors:

Donatella Barbieri, Sofia Pantouvaki, Suzanne Osmond)

Barbieri, Donatella, *Costume in Performance: Materiality, Culture, and the Body* (Bloomsbury Publishing, 2017)

Hann, Rachel, *Beyond Scenography* (Routledge, 2018)

Lehmann, Hans-Thies, *Postdramatic Theatre*, translated and with an introduction by Karen Jürs-Munby, (Routledge, 2006)

Lurie, Alison, *The Language of Clothes*, (Random House, 1st edition, 1981)

Maclaurin, Ali and Monks, Aoife, *Costume: Readings in Theatre Practice* (Red Globe Press, 2014 and Pelgrave, 2015)

Monks, Aoife, *The Actor in Costume* (Palgrave, 2009)

Sustainability

Jones, Ellen E., *A Practical Guide to Greener Theatre* (Routledge, 2013)

Kidao, Sinéad, *The Costume Directory* (BAFTA's Albert Consortium, 2016)

Beyond Design

Ingham, Rosemary and Covey, Elizabeth, *Costume Technician Handbook* (Heinemann Educational Books, 3rd edition, 2003)

Pride, Rebecca, *The Costume Supervisor's Toolkit: Supervising Theatre Costume Production from First Meeting to Final Performance*, (Focal Press Toolkit, 2018)

ONLINE RESOURCES

www.yorknotes.com (York Notes literature research)

www.sparknotes.com (Spark Notes literature research)

www.ecoscenography.com (on sustainability in theatre)

www.ecostagepledge.com (on sustainability in theatre)

www.broadwaygreen.com (on sustainability in theatre)

www.costumeagency.com (critical costume research)

www.angelsbehindtheseams.com (costume podcast)

Abstract: The Art of Design–Ruth E. Carter Costume Design (Netflix, 2019)

www.imdb.com (film credits and more)

www.theatredesign.org.uk (Society of British Theatre Designers)

www.bectu.org.uk (Broadcasting, Entertainment, Communications and Theatre Union)

www.bloomsburyfashioncentral.com

www.digitaltheatre.com (research hub)

www.learningonscreen.ac.uk (film and television archive)

www.behance.net (talent platform)

www.skillshare.com (learning platform)

LinkedIn learning (learning platform)

Facebook groups:

Set Swap Cycle
Costume Networking Group

Facebook offers many relevant groups that cater to specific niches and locations. It is good to keep in mind that a new Facebook group based on specific needs can always be started by anyone.

SECOND-HAND CLOTHING, FABRICS AND PATTERNS

www.minerva.com
www.clothspot.co.uk
www.tiaknightfabrics.co.uk
www.depop.com
www.onlineshop.oxfam.org.uk

www.whaleys-bradford.ltd.uk
www.friedmans.co.uk (wholesale)
www.clothhouse.com
www.fabricsgalore.co.uk
www.macculloch-wallis.co.uk
www.theberwickstreetclothshop.com
www.spoonflower.com

INDEX